T0146781

REFLECTIONS
AND OPINIONS
OF A MENTAL HEALTH
PROFESSIONAL 3

Henry C. Barbot, M.D.

Diplomat of the ABPN
(American Board of Psychiatry and Neurology)
Certified by the ASCP
(American Society of Clinical Psychopharmacology)
Diplomat of the ABAM
(American Board of Addiction Medicine)
Diplomat of the ABDA
(American Board of Disability Analysts)

authorHOUSE®

AuthorHouse™
1663 Liberty Drive
Bloomington, IN 47403
www.authorhouse.com
Phone: 1 (800) 839-8640

Published by AuthorHouse   02/08/2016

ISBN: 978-1-5049-7729-6 (sc)
ISBN: 978-1-5049-7731-9 (hc)
ISBN: 978-1-5049-7730-2 (e)

Library of Congress Control Number: 2016901807

Print information available on the last page.

This book is printed on acid-free paper.

CONTENTS

PREFACE

Will you be surprised, if I tell you that the journey started by Dr. Henry Claude Barbot, 3 years ago, with his fascinating book "REFLECTIONS AND OPINIONS OF A MENTAL HEALTH PROFESSIONAL", never stopped? There we go, with this time, his third volume, which will basically reconnect you to the subjects previously developed in his two former books. And certainly, Dr. Barbot added up a few new chapters, touching on many more captivating areas, which made this book frankly appealing.

Psychiatry is such a complex field, nevertheless indispensable and so challenging, leading to new adjustments every day, for a better understanding of the pathologic concepts and the treatments approach.

No wonder, Dr. Barbot, carefully, step by step, had navigated with us through some difficult areas of the Psychiatric specialty, such as anxiety disorders and their physical manifestations; the mood disorders, like in the case of "bipolar syndrome", psychosis and the somatic changes related to it, insanity and the serious problems associated with it, causing so much drama and pain in our society, and so on.

Think about it for a minute, and you realize right away, that psychiatric problems minor or major, are, whether we admit it or not, the core of our daily life. Often times, it is more comfortable to just ignore them, to avoid facing them and challenge them, as if they were just in our imagination. Unfortunately, they are real and should not just be dismissed, as if they were going away by themselves.

Let us not be foolish. The time has now come for everybody, especially the government to search and find a "modus operandi" to tackle seriously, the problems of mental illness and illicit substances, in the genesis of suicides and mass murders, when those deranged people unfortunately can get their hands on guns. This problem is becoming too familiar and more worrisome every day.

This book of course, will take you further, into some intricate areas, such as the emotional, physical and sexual abuse cases. Dr. Barbot will talk also about the influence of sex on the human brain and as well of the power of sex in intimate relationships; subjects that are, without any doubt, passionate and will for sure trigger your curiosity.

Overall, this book will amaze you, as you taking more and more interest in the psychiatric field. As you'll notice, there is even more to explore in it, for example the matter of suicide and the criminal justice system interaction. Interesting!

I am pleased to congratulate Dr. Henry Claude Barbot one more time, for a job so well done, and to recommend to the readers, to get the best out of such a wonderful book.

Dr. Jean Joseph Lochard, M.D.

INTRODUCTION

Dr. Barbot has done it again! He has taken his years of experience and encapsulated the wonders of the Human mind into his third book Reflections and Opinions of a Mental Health Professional 3.

In this third edition of the series, he relates to others in his field and the layman alike with real and provocative topics. Amongst the most controversial, he touches on the frequently occurring epidemic of young black males being terrorized and killed by white officers, suicide in the criminal justice system, and the influence of sex on the human brain. In addition, he offers us a special treat by delving into his own personal life outside of his work experience. Dr. Barbot gives us insight into his life as a Haitian man coming to America, and other personal writings relating to his innermost thoughts.

The pages of this addition are not just adorned with words from a mental health professional, but instead bleed of the knowledge, talent, and in depth writings of a dedicated expert in his craft. Every sentence, page, and chapter was composed meticulously and deliberately to convey a lasting message to the reader. Whether an average person or a seasoned doctor of psychiatry, there is indeed something for everyone within these pages. Comparable to the parent editions, Reflections and Opinions of a Mental Health Professional 3, bind us together in a fashion that we oftentimes try to escape. It presents the most intimate aspects of the human psyche in a primal and uncensored format that captures the good, the bad, and every tiny detail in between. Devised by a man with not only a profound understanding of the human mind, but an inherent passion for humanity, Dr. Barbot challenges us to see a side of mortality that is often misunderstood or masked with medical terminology and advanced jargon that we often dismiss as cover ups for a truth that we are not prepared to receive. Reflections and Opinions of a Mental Health Professional 3, is a bridge between the assumptions and the actuality of mental illness, the mind, and the everyday lives of those aggrieved with this emergent epidemic.

Claudine Barbot, Author &Playwright
"Through a Child's Eyes"
"From an Officer's Wife"

FOREWORD

In Dr. Henry Barbot's book "Reflections and Opinions of a Mental Health Professional 3," he gives a rare, direct, and informative look from his own observations. Leave it to the introspective writing skills of Dr. Barbot to delve deeper into topics many already presume as fully understood.

This is a carefully presented view from the knowledge and experiences of a serious health professional. He has a clear comprehension of the ever changing and continuously advancing field of psychiatry. He relentlessly provides a unique and personal perspective on disorders, society, and so much more.

He uses the illustration of *psycho somatic medicine* then proceeds to offer various examples to explain the association of the mind and body such as: IBS (Irritable bowel syndrome) and COPD's (chronic obstructive pulmonary disease) relation to anxiety. In the second chapter he lets us know how far back personality disorders go while naming a few early pioneers.

You will learn when liberation and sexual exploration are often used as a cover for deeper psychological addictions and disorders. In a time where it's less about what the doctor ordered and rather what the patient will listen to, his uncut opinion is exactly what we need. Dr. Barbot's passion for his occupation means you can feel his caring heart, see the wisdom reflected on the pages and hear the voice inside you whisper, "this is a brilliant read".

-Dr. Allen Gore, M.D. Psychiatrist

ACKNOWLEDGEMENT 3

The writing of my third book is for me like a blessing. Putting these books together in such a short period of time is a challenge. Coming to the US, I would never thought I would find myself in a medical field like Psychiatry which, I probably would never have chosen, had I stayed in Haiti. I am being humble about it, since I am helping and educating people about a discipline that carries a lingering stigma. As usual I credit my wife, my children, my brother in law, my sisters and my parents particularly the late Dr. Medrick P Barbot, M.D. for this additional achievement. I also want to add my great aunt Alina Blot, who raised me and was the first architect of my academic formation.

I will never forget that all these individuals were able to motivate me by the power, and the grace of God. At time I found myself with no creativity and confidence to tackle the issue in line. At time I question my qualifications in spite of the fact they have been tested so many times with outstanding results. However I still feel humble about it and ask God to guide me in the accomplishment of the difficult and challenging goals I impose on myself.

I am sure that under his guidance, I will reach the objective targeted with confidence.

04-05-15
Henry Claude Barbot, M.D.

AUTHOR'S NOTE 3

Like the first two volumes of this series, the third volume of "Reflections and Opinions of a Mental Health Professional", is a symbolic replica, a lively and vibrant representation of the years that I have spent practicing in the psychiatrics' arena. As I said so many times before, I consider myself a man who feels blessed honored and humble, by the privilege of dealing day in and day out with the "Human Mind" which could be so unpredictable, so explosive, at time so fragile, so resilient, and at time so vicious, so destructive and so incredibly callous, deadly and unscrupulous. I consider myself lucky to have some skills allowing me to have a sense of how treacherous and obnoxious our fellow human being can be. I am lucky to have some skills allowing me to have a sense of some individual's characters and subsequently having an ability to cope better with them.

This third version of the book: "Reflections and Opinions of a Mental Health Professional" 3, covers the same major categories listed in the first two books. The categories covered are:

In Chapter One: The Anxiety Disorders and some Anxiety Related Concepts. The titles discussed and developed are: "Anxiety Disorders and Physical illnesses" which emphasizes the relationship between the mind and the body. We have also covered: "Anxiety Disorders DSM-V version" describing how the new version of the DSM talks about Anxiety.

In Chapter Two, which deals with the personality disorders: "Personality Disorders, and Personality Development".

I describe just one title, which is developed at length and discussed under: "Personality Disorders and Personality Traits". This title as mentioned earlier, speaks at length about the history of the science behind the "Personality Disorders". The way this science was born, the way it progresses over time since the antiquity, even before the time of "Christ". We also talk about the contribution of some of the major players, who have made this science a powerful tool, helping in the identification of the human character, emphasizing the temperament of these individuals who live with us, are constantly around us and in our face, with all the potential for being unpredictable and possibly could cause all sort of nuisance by making our life a living hell.

This very important science about the study of people's character, that sheds some light by giving us some key clues about the temperament of the inhabitants of the jungle where we are all living as "Human Beings". "Human Beings" who are often transformed, metamorphosed into "Wild Animals" preying at each other.

In Chapter Three: "Universal Concepts". This title that covers the "XXIst Century" goes through the major and important issues of this century, all the positives and all the negatives about this period of time, and the transition between this century and the one before. In Chapter three there is also a piece entitled "Alteration" describing how human beings have a tendency to alter "Change" over time, and how in a way this characteristic is an integral part of their nature.

In Chapter Four, the chapter on "Forensics Concepts" The book describes some titles like: "Suicide and the Criminal Justice System", "The profound analogy between Terrorists and Mass Murderers secondary to Mental Illnesses". "Reflections and Opinions" goes into a detailed description of the timing and the modus operandi of suicides in Us Jails and Prisons. It emphasizes the major stressors leading to suicide for people in sequestration. People who are in seclusion usually deal with a lot of stressors including: a loss of liberty, a high degree of enforced structure and discipline, dealing with the guilt and shame associated with their situation, along with the impact of incarceration on their family.

In Chapter Five, The chapter on "Geriatrics Concepts", the titles discussed: "The never ending conflict between Youth and Old Age, or Stupidity Versus Maturity" reflects how we probably will never stop comparing the way we felt when we were twenty and the way we feel now. In other word we perhaps will never stop comparing our naivety and our stupidity of yesterday to our maturity and wisdom of today. This will probably go on, our entire life. In the other segment described under: "When will we stop mourning our youth?" ; we could have a sense of how some of us will never stop mourning our youth. Some of us will never stop fantasizing about having an eternal life or a youth, which will never end.

Chapter Six, the chapter on "Sleep an sleep related Concepts", "Reflections and Opinions" will continue its digging on the mysteries of Sleep. The book will continue its attempts on shedding some light on this puzzling and intriguing phenomenon, represented by our "Sleep". The book will describe the similarity between the deep reversible stages of "sleep" and the deep irreversible state of lethargy of "death". It will focus on the chilling, creepy, petrifying feeling experienced by our relatives when they are unable to awake us or retrieve us from the deepest stage of our sleep. We really "look dead", it really seems like we have reached the terminus of the organic material's life expectancy. This stage that is feared by most of us unless we paradoxically request and seem to enjoy it under certain circumstances. Titles like: "The profound analogy between Sleep and Death" illustrates the previous comments. Other title such as "The wonders of Sleep Study" will continue to display our fascination with the phenomenon of sleep, and will justify our attempts to know more about the subject, by exploring the fascinating aspect of the science behind it. The piece described as the "Marvels of sleep Study and sleep Pharmacology" goes through some of the most recent discoveries in the field. "Sleep disorders as per DSM-5" describes and classifies sleep disorders as per the new DSM.

In chapter Seven, The chapter on: "Culture and Cultural Matter", "Reflections and Opinions" by commenting on some titles such as: "The powerful impact of Culture on people life style" and "Culture and Mental Health Diagnosis", will emphasize the importance of our culture on our way of living our life, our philosophy about life and our way of communicating with one another. This chapter also describes under "The possession phenomenon in the Voodoo Religion" which is probably one of the most puzzling feature of the voodoo religion. In "Haitian Mentality" the books describes one the vicissitude of the "Haitian Society" which is in realty a phenomenon observed almost everywhere, therefore it is more of an universal occurrence.

Going through Chapter Eight, The chapter on "Developmental Matter", by developing some title like: "Is Adolescence synonymous with getting berserk"?

The book focuses on the anatomical and physiological aspect of the Adolescent brain to explain the psychological and psychodynamic aspect of his behavior.

In chapter Nine, the chapter on "Mind over Matter", "Reflections and Opinions" comment on the unlimited power of the mind and how it could allow us to accomplish anything we really strive for. Title like: "The power of the mind and the Survival Instinct" reflect an incredibly powerful combination allowing Human Beings to achieve what could be perceived as impossible.

Moving to Chapter Ten, the chapter on "Biological Concepts", "Reflections and Opinions of a mental Health Professional" focuses on a many different titles like: "Psychiatric Disorders and Medical Illnesses", "Street Drugs and Medical Illnesses",

"Scattered thoughts on Addiction Medicine", "The hazard associated with Psychotropic Medications", "The Pluses and Minuses of the New DSM".

In "Psychiatric Disorders and medical Illnesses" we review a large variety of medical illnesses that manifest as if we were dealing with some psychiatric conditions. Acute Renal Failure by example can manifest exactly as an acute psychotic nosology.

Some psychotropic medications could induce a large variety of hazardous conditions such as "NMS" or "Neuroleptic Malignant Syndrome" and the "Serotonin Syndrome".

In "Scattered thoughts in Addiction Medicine", the Book reviews a large number of drug intoxication and a description of their negative impact on the body. In the poem named the "Pluses and the Minuses of the new DSM" the book emphasized that, may be the largest deficiency of the new DSM is its getting rid of the "five axis diagnostic strategy" and its amazing ability to summarize a large number of data for a psychiatric patient. In addition "Reflections and opinions of a Mental Health Professional 3" incorporates in this chapter on "biological Concepts" some other fascinating segments such as: "Pseudo Bulbar Affect and Traumatic Brain injury", "Varenicline" another option for the treatment of Alcohol Dependence, "The use of Gapapentin for Alcohol Dependence", "Cannabis and abnormalities of the Nucleus Acumbens and the Amygdala In the Youth", "Prescribed Medications and False Positivity during Drug Testing", "Transcranial Near-Infrared Therapy, a new Neuro-Modulation technic for Depression" and finally "The Biological aspect of Depression and Suicide"

In Chapter eleven which is the chapter dedicated to "Human Interaction", "Reflections and Opinions" focuses on the heavy weight of Human interaction in "Modern Clinical Psychiatry" in the following title: "The strength and weaknesses of Human Interaction"

Chapter Twelve, the Chapter on "Emotional, Sexual and Abusive Relationships", by going through title like: "The perpetuity of Emotional, Sexual and Physical Abuse in Human Beings", reveals or better displays a picture where all categories of abuses could be included and how they could impact a vulnerable mind. It portrays some specimen who, by being in profound denial, end up embracing their abusers, identifying with them, perceiving them falsely instead as protectors, and attributing them with all sorts of virtues that depict them as their soul mates. These soul mates, who in reality are nothing but disgusting and unscrupulous individuals who are profiting from their naivety and their ignorance to exploit their body, their spirit and their naivety, transforming them into sex slaves and sex addicts.

Moving on with our exploration of the different chapters of this third version of "Reflections and opinions", Chapter Thirteen, the Chapter on "Psychotherapy and Psychotherapy Subtypes" describes some specific types of therapy such as: "Interpersonal Therapy" or ITP, a modality of therapy targeting specifically some "Depressive Disorders". This psychotherapeutic approach was described by: Myrna Weissman and Gerald Klerman. These authors smartly realize that one of the major weakness of these mood disorders, in other word their Achilles's heel, is a flaw in interpersonal behavior, leaving the depressed individual with feelings of loneliness, abandonment and isolation.

Another psychotherapeutic approach described in this chapter, targets individuals suffering from "Borderline Personality Disorder". This particular approach Known as "Dialectic Behavioral Therapy" was designed and developed by Martha Lineham. This is a subtype of "Cognitive behavioral Therapy", which targets a constellation of symptoms that are well known in the "Borderline Patient". These symptoms are of different quality or variety; they are: emotional "Affective Instability", behavioral "Self Injurious Behavior", interpersonal "Evaluation and Devaluation of Others". This chapter also includes a third variety of therapy "Motivational Therapy" and describes how this psychotherapeutic approach can do wonders in patients suffering from Substance use and dependence by in absence of coercion. The key is not put any pressure on these patients who are already ambivalent about going to treatment and let them decide freely.

Continuing the exploration of the content of "reflections and Opinions of a Mental Health Professional 3", by moving to Chapter

Fourteen, the chapter on" "Sex and Sexual Disorders" which focuses on this title: "The power of Sex on intimate relationships" describing how Sex could be the nutrient, the food necessary for the longevity of intimate relationships. This chapter also talks about: "The influence of Sex on the Human Brain" a really captivating and educational Topic, that probably will make us a better sexual partners for our mates. In the same chapter there is a section reflecting the description of "Sexual Disorders according to DSM-5".

Chapter Fifteen, the chapter on "Psychosis and Psychotic Concepts" develops titles like: "Psychosis, Insanity and the Human mind" and "Psychotic Disorders DSMV version".

Chapter Sixteen, the chapter on "Mood Disorder and Mood related Concepts" talks about: "Mood Disorders success and survival" and: "Mood Disorders DSMV version".

Chapter Seventeen which focuses on: "Personal and Professional Matter" depicting some titles Like: "The Sudden Collapse of my Universe", "Is Retirement still a possible option in this day and age?","My Haitian journey, Vs. My American journey" and a self-psychoanalysis: "Weakness of Character or being hostile and wild".

Finally Chapter Eighteen, the last chapter of this book, focuses as usual on Miscellaneous themes reflected in headings such as: "The Fruits of the Haitian Countryside", "The Haitian Industry", "The Harvest of the Sugar Cane", "Rural Festivity", "You" a segment reflecting the description of the creepy relationship between some parents and their children in Haiti in the late 60's. "Riviere Froide" talks about the description of a region considered as a heaven on earth, an idyllic site for the numerous lovers of our land. Ultimately a segment named: "The influence of Music on the Human Brain" which is another educational piece, depicting the magical influence of Music on our brain.

H.C.B

05-25-15

Chapter 1: Anxiety and Anxiety related Concepts

_Anxiety Disorders and Physical Illnesses

_Anxiety Disorders DSM-V version

Anxiety Disorders and Physical Illnesses

There is a connection between anxiety and physical illnesses.

This does not seem surprising, since we know there is a relationship between the mind and the body.

Some physical conditions like Asthma are often linked to anxiety.

Anxiety can indeed affect different systems in our body including the following: The CNS (Central Nervous System), the CVS (Cardio Vascular System), the GIS (Gastro Intestinal System), the RS (Respiratory System) and the GUS (Genito Urinary System) to name a few. This is an illustration of the so-called "Psycho Somatic Medicine", in other word the impact of the psyche on the body.

What follows is a small group of medical illnesses commonly associated with anxiety: IBS (Irritable Bowel Syndrome), Hyperthyroidism, CAD (Coronary Artery Disease), COPD (Chronic Obstructive Pulmonary disease) and Asthma.

Considering IBS, the most frequent symptoms associated with this condition are: crampy abdominal pain, bloating, diarrhea, gas accumulation, food intolerance, and bouts of anxiety.

Moving to heart diseases, anxiety can induce some symptoms such as: crushing chest pain, sometime, it could be with or without ischemia or with normal coronary arteries. It could also induce or come simultaneously with some subtypes of cardiac arrhythmia, creating mayhem on the sufferer. A typical example would be PAT

(Paroxysmal Atrial Tachycardia) or AF (Atrial Fibrillation) when the subject feels like his heart is about to jump out of his chest. This could also be bidirectional, like what usually happen in a 2 way street. Once the Paroxysmal Atrial tachycardia is treated, the symptoms of anxiety resolve or diminish. Or it could be the opposite; once the anxiety subsides the cardiac condition seems more manageable.

It is astonishing to see how stress or emotional disturbances go hand-in-hand with certain medical conditions. It can even trigger them. Hyperthyroidism is a classic paradigm; its onset could be sudden and seems to follow some stressful event or some emotional crisis.

Or it could be the reverse, emotional turmoil at the time of onset could possibly be the product of an early and unsuspected thyroid over-activity; some degree of emotional instability characterizes some subjects with Hyperthyroidism.

In order to differentiate a primary medical nosology from one induced by anxiety, one must in some cases confirm it by ordering some lab works such as: TSH (Thyroid Stimulating Hormone), an ECG (Electro cardiography), or some radio imaging such as a Chest-Xray among others.

All of these features described earlier, remind one of the clinical presentation of certain maladies born from the impact of anxiety on some medical disorders.

This is a snapshot, a thumbnail allowing one to have a glimpse of the phenomenology of anxiety and its influence on a small group of medical disorders.

H.C.B

01-24-15

Anxiety Disorders DSMV version

When we describe the anxiety disorders according to the new version of the DSM, some of them such as "Separation Anxiety Disorder" are seen both in children and in adults even if they are for the most part, illnesses that are seen more frequently during childhood.

"Separation Anxiety Disorder" is defined as a developmentally inappropriate, an excessive fear or anxiety concerning the separation from those to whom the individual is attached.

This is also an ailment in which the sufferer experiences recurrent excessive distress when he is distant from home, away from some major attachment figures.

The patient is concerned about the wellbeing or even the death of these attachment figures that are away from him. He has a need to know their where about and yearns to stay in touch with them. In addition he ruminates about untoward events falling on their idols, such as getting lost or being kidnapped; or having some fatalities that would keep him from ever being reunited with the object of his obsession.

In children this condition may be comorbid with "General Anxiety Disorder" or "Specific Phobia", while in Adult it is likely to be associated with almost every single anxiety disorders including: "Specific Phobia", "Post Traumatic Stress Disorder", "Panic Disorder", "General Anxiety Disorder", "Social Anxiety Disorder" and "Obsessive Compulsive Disorder". It could also be comorbid with some "Personality Disorder" or some "Mood Disorder".

The DSMV also describes "Selective Mutism" a condition often marked by a high degree of social anxiety. The lack of speech often occurs in social interaction. "Selective Mutism" is often linked with excessive shyness, fear of social embarrassment, social isolation, negativism, clinging, temper tantrum, or some mild oppositional behavior.

Another condition listed by the new DSM Is "Specific Phobia", which is an irrational fear of what seems like every single entity on earth. This condition was described in the second volume of Reflections and Opinions Of a Mental Health Professional under: "Universal Fear". DSMV talks about "Social Anxiety Disorder" also described in the second volume of this series under: "The Pathetic Performer" a condition that leads the patient to become terrorized in certain social situation.

The new DSM went on to talk about Panic Disorder a condition that is like a catastrophic event for the sufferer who really thinks he is about to die by having a dreadful condition like a heart Attack.

DSMV progresses in its description of the Anxiety Disorders by talking about General Anxiety Disorder, which was also described in the first volume of our series under: "Inborn Worriers"

The new DSM also talk about Obsessive Compulsive and related Disorders which has under its umbrella such entities like "Obsessive Compulsive Disorder" (OCD), "Body Dysmorphic Disorder", "Hoarding Disorder", "Trichotillomania", "Excoriation Disorder" Known also under "Skin Picking Disorder", "Substance /Medication induced Obsessive Compulsive Disorder", "Obsessive Compulsive Disorder due to another medical condition", "Body-Focused Repetitive Behavior Disorder", "Obsessional Jalousie"

The Key components of these disorders are Obsession and Compulsion. Obsession is defined as recurrent and persistent thoughts, urges, images experienced as intrusive and unwanted whereas Compulsions are repetitive behaviors or mental acts that a person feels driven to perform in response to an obsession or according to rules that must be applied rigidly. Other conditions in this category are characterized primarily by recurrent body-focused repetitive behavior (Hair Pulling, Skin Picking) as well as repeated attempt to decrease or stop the behaviors.

The DSM V includes another cluster of anxiety disorders known under the denomination of "Trauma and Stressors Related Disorders" like "Reactive Attachment Disorder", "Disinhibited Social Engagement Disorder", "Post Traumatic Stress Disorder" (PTSD), "Acute Stress Disorder" and "Adjustment Disorders" a condition described under the denomination of: "The Burden of Adaptation": in the second volume of Reflections and Opinions of a Mental Health Professional.

This is a review of the classification of the "Anxiety Disorders" as perceived and described by the new DSM.

H.C.B

08-10-15

Chapter 2: Personality and Personality Development

_ Personality Disorders
and Personality Traits

Personality Disorders and Personality Traits

According to certain sources, the study of characters or personality disorders goes back to the antiquity even "Before Christ". This is a longer period of time that we would imagine.

These personality disorders used to be divided, in the fourth century before Christ, in 30 different subtypes. The characters described then seem to have a strong influence on subsequent studies of human personality.

Thomas Overbury (1581-1613) in England and Jean de la Bruyere (1645-1696) in France are considered pioneers in the field. They also had a tremendous influence in the framework of personality disorders as they are conceived today.

The concept of personality disorder itself is reportedly more recent and dates back to the French psychiatrist Philippe Pinet in his 1801 description of "Manie Sans Delire", characterized by outburst of rage and violence, in the absence of any psychotic illness components or concepts such as delusions and hallucinations.

About 60 years later it was reported in 1896 that, the German psychiatrist Emile Kreapelin (1856 -1926) described 7 forms of antisocial behavior under the denominations of "Psychopathic Personalities". This was broadened later by a colleague of kraepelin, Kurt Schneider (1887-1967) who wrote a seminal volume of "Psychopathic Personalities" in 1923; that still form the basic of current classifications of personality disorders as described by the "DSMIV".

These personality disorders are described as, an enduring pattern of inner experiences and behavior that deviates markedly from what is expected culturally. In addition there is generally an inflexible and pervasive pattern, beginning in adolescence or early adulthood that remains stable overtime and triggers distress and impairment.

We know by example that, DSMIV described ten personality disorders, which are themselves divided in clusters.

"Cluster A" gathers the odd, "bizarre and eccentric individuals" and includes in its rank: the "Paranoid", the "Schizoid" and the "Schizotypal".

"Cluster B" for its parts assembles the "dramatic and erratic folks", and talks about the "Antisocial", the "Borderline", the "Histrionic" and the "Narcissistic".

"Cluster C" which is the last cluster described in this group, compiles the "anxious and fearful people", and focuses on the "Avoidant", the "Dependent" and the "Obsessive compulsive".

Some people, who are deeply involved and studied at length the personality disorders, think these findings are more the product of "historical observation" rather than some "scientific studies".

These people often thought these results could be in reality some vague and imprecise concepts, since they at time tend to blur into one another with no clear delineation. They indeed do overlap at time. As a rule of thumb, most people with personality disorders never saw a psychiatrist or any other mental health professional for that matter.

Going through the different members of the "Cluster A".

The "Paranoid" is characterized by a pervasive distrust of others including friends and partners. He is usually guarded and suspicious and is constantly scanning his environment in the search of clues or suggestions confirming his fears. In addition these individuals have a sense of self-importance and personal right. They are also very sensitive to setbacks and easily feel shames and humiliations; they constantly bear grudges as well. They do withdraw from other people and usually if not always, avoid engaging in close relationships.

The "Schizoid" has a naturel tendency to direct his attention toward his inner world and away from the external world. He is detached and aloof and is frequently prone to introspection and fantasy. He has no desire for social and sexual relationship and is indifferent to the external world, which is reflected in his lack of emotional response. He could even appear cold and callous. He usually is not perceived as needing any form of treatment since he is able to function at his own capacity. He has a rich inner life, since this is what is important for him. He does not have any concern about society in general and the external world around him. He does not long for intimacy since for him initiating and maintaining interpersonal relationships is too difficult and too distressing. That is why he feels so comfortable retreating in his inner world.

The "Schizotypal" is unique in his characterization. As a group they are usually bizarre in their appearance, their behavior and their speech. They do have some anomalies of thinking similar to a schizophrenic patient such as of odds beliefs, magical thinking, suspiciousness, obsessional rumination and unusual perceptual experiences. They do have a high probability to become schizophrenics. They even call them sometime "Latent Schizophrenics".

Moving on to the "Cluster C" and targeting: The "Antisocial" a type of personality disorder which is more common in men than in women is characterized by a callous individual, who is unconcerned by the feelings of others. He usually disregards social rules and obligations. He is obnoxious, irritable aggressive, impulsive and guilt lacking. He does not usually have any difficulties findings relationships and can be superficially charming and is sometime called "The charming psychopath". I personally call them the "Impersonated gentlemen" and a section was reserved to them in the chapter on personality disorders of the second volume of this series. They generally have a criminal record and could be in and out of jails, an environment very familiar to them.

The "Borderline", who is the second notorious member of this group, usually lacks a sense of self and has no identity and is overwhelmed by some feelings of emptiness and some fear of being abandon. He usually has a pattern of intense but unstable relationship. He often exhibits some emotional instability with outburst of anger, violence and impulsive behavior. One of his hallmarks is suicidal threats and acts of self-harm.

As a group, they were named "Borderline" because they originally thought they were at the border between psychotic and neurotic disorders. Their condition is often linked from childhood sexual abuse and is more common in women, who are more likely to be the victims of childhood sexual abuse. I usually consider them as deeply emotional and volcanic and I call them "Tormented Souls" as described in the first volume of this series.

The third member of this cluster usually called "The Histrionic" usually lacks a sense of self-worth and depends on others for attention and approval. He also tends to be melodramatic as if he was playing a role. He could be very manipulative and is often seeking for attention. He takes great care of his physical appearance and is overly charming and inappropriately seductive. He is at time a victim of exploitations. He also seems insincere and superficial in his romantic relationships. This is quite distressing for him, since he is sensitive to criticisms and rejections and reacts badly to losses and failures.

The "Narcissistic" comes from the myth of Narcissus who was a beautiful youth who fell in love with his own reflection. He has a grandiose sense of self, a sense of self- importance, self-entitlement and a need to be admired. He does not have empathy and he is ready to exploit others to achieve his goal. He is usually self-absorbed, controlling, intolerant selfish and insensitive. When he feels slighted or ridicule, he may have a fit of destructive anger and is revenge seeking. Such a "narcissistic rage" often follows a "narcissistic injury" and can have disastrous consequence. The narcissistic patient is also described in the first Volume of "Reflections and Opinions of a Mental Health Professional" under the title "Entitlement".

Describing the last cluster or "Cluster C" with the "Avoidant", the "Dependent" and the "Obsessive Compulsive".

We will start with the "Avoidant" who is generally persistently tense because of his belief of being socially inept unappealing or inferior. As a result he has a fear of being embarrassed, criticized or rejected. He often avoids meeting people unless he is certain of being liked. He is restrained even in his intimate relationship and avoids taking risks. The Avoidant personality is strongly associated with anxiety disorder. Psycho-dynamically it may be associated with actual or perceived rejection by parents or peers during childhood.

The "Dependent" usually has a lack of self- confidence and does have an excessive need to be taken care of. He needs help making daily routine decision and often depends on others to make important life decisions on his behalf. He has a fear of abandonment and may go the extra mile to secure and maintain relationships. He sees himself as inadequate and helpless; therefore gives up personal responsibility to others he idealizes as being competent or powerful. People from the cluster B Group, who are flattered by the high regard they are being held because of the dependent self-effacing role, often dominate the Dependent patient.

The "Obsessive–Compulsive patient is usually characterized by an excessive preoccupation with details, rules, lists, organizations and schedules. His perfectionism usually prevents him from finishing a task. He is devoted to work and productivity at the expense of leisure and relationships. He is doubting and controlling, humorless and miserly. His high level of anxiety arises from a perceived lack of control over his universe, which is escaping between his fingers and puzzles him. As a consequence, he does have little tolerance for grey area and would rather simplify his universe by perceiving actions or beliefs absolutely right or absolutely wrong, therefore allowing him to have a better grasp on it. His relationship with people closed to him is usually strained because of the unreasonable and inflexible demands he place on them.

This snapshot on personality disorders is an analytic exploration, a roaming made with the purpose of having a sense of the character, the maladaptive, solidly engrained personality traits we commonly find in people we usually meet every day, people who live with us and around us, and for whom we do not have any clue of what they are up to, or what they are capable of doing to us. Having placed them and their character under the microscope, we will probably be able to have an idea of the profoundly ingrained, deeply buried childhood experiences that could later blossom into personality traits or disorders. These experiences could possibly allow us to perceive the world in a more objective way and make it possibly a better place, since we will have a sense of what to expect from people who are constantly around us days in and days out.

H.C.B

02-15-15

Chapter 3:
Universal Concepts

_ XX.th & XX1st Century

_ Alteration

The Twentieth and Twenty-first Century

These are the centuries of major changes, they are "revolutionary centuries"; this is how some of us perceive them. Others see them, as a total degradation of all moral values, a true shutdown of all ethics rules. Even though orgies and sexual liberation have been seen before, even though they probably have been around forever, they were not perceived as blatantly as they are now.

Moving to Drugs and alcohol, they seem to be the turning point and dominate most individuals during this era, controlling their lives by making them so addicted to these compounds that become as precious to them as the air they are breathing. It is as if the natural enjoyments, the delights most of us usually are satisfied by, do not exist anymore. It is as if certain activities such as: working out and sexual intercourse to name a few become nonexistent. People are ingurgitating, killing themselves with all kinds of street drugs such as: Cocaine, PCP, Marijuana, Amphetamine, Methamphetamine, Opioids, and a large group of "designer drugs" like K2, bath salts to name a couple. Nowadays the public would rather be addicted to these drugs, than getting involved in some healthy activities that probably would be more natural and pleasurable.

These epochs have also brought many new ways of perceiving life, the definition of marriage by example, which used to be a sacred union between a man and a woman, has changed profoundly. Nowadays same-sex individuals are happily and officially united.

There are also some scary dreadful unspeakable events that did invade these Centuries. This is the period that has seen the birth of terrorism, considered as the most horrifying and atrocious strategies to destroy human lives. They do engage in extensive devastation and demolition of properties in addition to their regularly periodic carnage. They will not hesitate doing any devilish misdeed to achieve their goal of creating mayhem, ruin and destruction of lives and property. They would go to the extreme of attaching some explosive devices to their body, and blow themselves up becoming "suicide bombers". By so doing they become deeply engaged in the practice of their religion and think they will become martyrs after their death.

This period have also seen a growing population of "bonafide psychopaths and sociopaths", individuals who seem different from the ordinary mentally ill. They seem to have reached some extreme in the chaotic state of their mind, making them much more dangerous than the typical mentally ill patient. These psychopaths who engage in horrific, unspeakable mass or serial killing, are often compared to the terrorists and some people often wonder whether there is a difference between the terrorists and these deeply deranged individuals. These specimen seem to be a new race of individuals, a new group of sick characters, growing like mushrooms almost everywhere in the world. Some of them exploit their status as being mentally ill, to claim a standing of being "Non Guilty By Reason of Insanity" (NGRI), in an attempt to get away with their hideous crime.

Another aspect of these two centuries is that they are considered as the birth, the growth and the explosion of electronics. This electronic invasion comes across as a volcanic eruption invading people's lives and killing their privacy. This is probably one of the prices we all have to pay for being gratified by this heavy rain of new technology, possibly creating an inundation in our life along with some collateral damages. There is indeed an explosion of items born in this epoch, which is really the age of technology. We have seen the appearance of: "the smart phones", "the iPods", "the tablets" and all these tiny wonders, born in this era of wireless technology. This age could be also named, the "centuries of blue tooth technology".

With this afflux of devices, also comes the death of family relationship. These warm feelings of family interaction, so comforting to most of us are probably the biggest losses of this epoch. Social media is slowly replacing them and is building an artificial biosphere to replace them.

If one observes family interaction in this day and age, family members hardly interact with each other since they are too busy playing with their electronic toys. They are too engrossed and fascinated by these gadgets to acknowledge each other. This is probably the price to pay for these new age devices: "The killing of family attachment and closeness".

In addition these tiny marvels can cause a total loss of privacy, since they could also spy on us by giving our exact location, anytime to anyone who would like to have this information.

H.C.B

05-30-15

Alteration

Human beings generally like changes.

In a way this characteristic is an integral part of their nature.

Since they keep modifying, altering themselves constantly in their evolution.

They seem to enjoy change, variation, and amendment because monotony prevents them from breathing while ongoing constant modification allows them to blossom.

They are suffocated by sameness, may be because as stated previously, in their evolution they went through different phases.

They went from one stage to the other in a systematic and methodic way.

They are initially conceived by forming the so-called "Egg or Zygote" during the zygotic phase, which is a result of the fusion of a spermatozoid and an ovule.

During the next phase they develop and progress to the embryonic stage and become "an embryo".

Throughout the following stages the transformation progresses and they finally become a full fledge "fetus".

This fetus subsequently becomes a newborn after labor. This newborn continues to grow, he keeps changing, going through various phases of development, until a hormonal explosion showers him, when he reaches "Adolescence", one of the most significant stage of Human evolution.

However what comes across as a pattern of variation, a constant tendency toward modification that seems innate, stays over time with the human being and keeps growing, budding consistently with him.

This is perhaps the reason why, the "Homo Sapiens", the human being is relentlessly searching, endlessly trying to evade, escape his usual habitual environment.

This may also be perceived as a way to replenish his source of energy and vivify him.

What seems to be like a second nature, a habit of staying in constant motion in order to get rid of any potential lethargy and tedious feeling, is being reflected in many aspects of his life, which is often unbalanced and unpredictable.

This could also be one of the reasons why he is frequently attracted by new adventures, or more generally any form of novelty.

This could possibly be one of the reasons the "unknown", the "X factor" often attracts him.

Furthermore this unknown entity has lost all its appeal all its attraction, once it has become acknowledged.

This unknown element has lost its magical charm, its fascination, its magnetism; simply because it has become more usual, more acknowledged more "recognized" or "known".

It has changed its status of being unknown to becoming routine and familiar. As a result of the change, his interest for it has completely gone, vanished, disappeared in a heartbeat. The elimination of the "x factor" makes it tedious, boring, dull and unattractive to him.

Henry C. Barbot, M.D.

This is one more time the negative influences of the spontaneous attraction Human Beings appear to have for changes, renovations, and amendments or "alterations".

This is in other word how alteration can impact us as Human Beings.

H.C.B.
Translated from French
07-27-15

Chapter 4:
Forensics Concepts

_Suicides and the Criminal Justice System

_The profound analogy between
Terrorists and Mass Murderers

Suicides and the Criminal Justice System

The reason why there is an elevated rate of suicides in the criminal justice system, particularly in jails and prisons is probably because the incarcerated population is dealing with some major stressors.

Among the stressors documented or recognized, it has been observed that these people usually deal with: a "loss of liberty", a high degree of "enforced structure and discipline", "overcrowding" and a "dirty, depressed and aggressive environment"; in addition to "poor diet", "feeling of guilt and shame".

What make the situation worse, are a power differential between incarcerated individuals and institutional staffs, and an uncertain future.

Coping with the impact of incarceration on important others (children, spouse, family), could be torture, agony for these individuals.

For the geriatric people who have dealt with factors such as "substance abuse" and "homelessness", things seem even tougher.

This group of inmates considered geriatric when they are older than 50, the large majority 75% have major problems with substance abuse, particularly alcohol upon incarceration. Most of these persons, 75% are incarcerated for violent offenses (rapes, sexual assaults). May be worse of all, 85% have serious chronic medical conditions such as HTN (Hypertension), Maturity Onset

Diabetes, COPD (Chronic Obstructive Pulmonary Disease) and CHF (Congestive Heart Failure).

They also have to deal with some internal factors, such as: violence or lack of respect from younger, stronger inmates, lack of privacy and appropriate accommodations (access to bathroom facilities), noisy environment, lack of friendships, a desire to be housed with similar aged inmates and a lack of space and poor ventilation.

These subjects have to deal with long sentences for repeat offenders and usually have prevalent mental illnesses at age 60 or above, including: substance abuse, dementia, antisocial personality, schizophrenia, borderline intellectual functioning and major depressive disorder. The worse they could ever have to deal with is at their release from custody, they have to confront some difficulties with placement, when they are being rejected by some facilities for their history of violence, which could be a major blow for them.

Another scenario is when some family members may be resistant or unable to provide care for them or may be worse, are no longer living.

This is not the end of their nightmares since they are often facing difficulties with employability, personal adjustment and following up care. We then can understand why as a rule, incarceration increases the risks for suicide, suicidal and Para suicidal behavior.

Suicides are responsible for 6% of deaths in prisons and 30% of death in jail. County Jails reportedly have a suicide rate at 4 folds above the rate for the general population. This suicide rate is most prevalent in younger 18 years of age, older above 35 year and white males above 55 years of age; these subjects are deemed to be at higher risks.

The other sadly important statistics to emphasize are that: about 25% of suicide, occur during the first 24 hours of incarceration; 50%

occur during the first week and 65% during the first 6 months or 180 days.

Hanging is usually the most successful suicide method; which usually is in about 80% of cases according to certain data, and occur inside the cell.

This somber and dread scenario is draconic enough for most people to the point, they will probably do whatever they possibly can, in order to stay away from the criminal justice system.

H.C.B

01-19-15

The profound analogy between Terrorists and Mass Murderers

Is there a difference between a terrorist, a mass murderer and a psychopath?

There is probably no difference at all, since for the most part the end result is the same.

They all seem to carry the same cold- blooded resolve, in order to achieve their dirty deed without an iota of remorse whatsoever. They all seem to go on with their lives as if nothing has ever happened; they carry on eating, joking, fornicating, shitting and with all other activities and aspects of life, as if they have not done anything wrong, as if all these lives lost, gone forever, were not the product of their action.

They just don't have a conscience; they just do not give a shit about killing a large number of innocent people.

These massive losses of lives do not matter to them. They allow themselves to decide arbitrarily on people's destiny as if they were God, as if they had the power to procreate; therefore thinking that also gives them the right to dispose of people's fate.

They have said time and time again that mentally ill individuals by and large are not violent, as a rule they are generally not considered as criminals. However no one can say the same for the psychopath, who scientifically is considered as cold-blooded individuals who do their repugnant deed with no remorse.

Osama Bin Laden, the mastermind of the tragedy hitting the United Stated on September 11, 2001, was euphoric after he learned that his plan so carefully concocted, was a complete success. He was so euphoric after he learned that the plan of massive destruction elaborated by his sick mind was a complete success. His demonic and evil plan that created mayhem in a lot, a multitude of people's lives, with massive destruction of property and uncountable losses of life with total decimation of family unity. This plan elaborated by such a cynical and evil mind; a plan so satanic that it does not have any justification whatsoever.

A plan that not even the conflicted philosophy opposing the major super powers of the world could justify. No philosophy on earth indeed can justify this large-scale carnage, this outrageous mega-scale massacre. No rational on earth, even the commonly called "American Imperialism" or the so-called "Anti- Imperialism" adopted by some "Socialism-Communism Countries" could explain or justify.

This is "pure psychopathy", this is pure unadulterated insanity, and this is the pure product of a criminally insane mind. This clearly exhibits, clearly displays that there is no demarcation, not even an iota of difference but pure unchangeable analogy between a terrorist, a mass murderer and a psychopath.

H.C.B

05-23-15

Chapter 5:
Geriatrics Concepts

_The never ending Conflict between Youth and Old Age or Stupidity Vs. Maturity

_When will we stop mourning our Youth?

The never-ending conflict between youth and senescence, or stupidity vs. cleverness

It seems like Youth and Old age symbolize two different worlds, two different universes.

We will probably never forget the splendor of our Youth when we reach Old age.

When comparing our physical appearance during the early part of our life to our look at the dusk or the crepuscule of it, this evaluation seems similar to the description of the notion of day vs. night.

We generally feel so confident during our youth that we foolishly think we can accomplish and overcome every single task or object coming our way. We do have a feeling of invincibility that seems to erode as we become older and start weighing our options.

We put almost every single entity under scrutiny as we age. We gage our stamina and our potential for success with caution instead of jumping blindly into an uncertain and adventurous leap with no guaranty of achieving our goals.

We wisely choose to slowly secure our moving on solid ground.

We wisely scan our environment and later compare our having no regard for our health at the dawn of our life to our state of constant fretfulness concerning our well being as we age.

Henry C. Barbot, M.D.

Our brain becomes clever and our temperament matures as we become older compared to the stupidity and the impulsivity of our childhood.

All these circumlocutions are to say that most of us can't help being trapped in a never-ending conflict between our youth and our senescence, our being stupid and immature versus our cleverness and wisdom.

H.C.B

08-15-15

When will we stop mourning our youth?

Will we ever stop mourning our youth?

When we focus on the passage of time, giving it too much attention, we realize how slow it could be.

However when we do not pay it any mind, we come to the realization of how fast it could also be.

It could be so fast that it becomes really alarming.

It frightens us and scares the living hell out of us.

It worries us extremely since with the passage of time, we continue to look, feel and act different.

Our anatomic structures turn out to be different.

Our bones become more fragile and are overwhelmed by all kinds of arthritic conditions.

Our joints and our tendons, become stiff losing their pliability, losing all their elasticity making us unable to move around the way we used to.

Our blood vessels become clogged because of all the material deposed in their wall and, depending of which vessel is being affected; this could provoke a cardiac arrest, a stroke, an intermittent claudication or a shot down of our kidneys.

All the possibilities quoted could be a direct consequence of their clogging and the resulting inability to feed our organs.

The most vital organs usually cannot cope with the obstruction and die either gradually or suddenly.

Fat takes over making it difficult to drag our body, making it impossible for us to ambulate.

We become obese and our body mass index goes through the roof.

The refine features of our body that usually make us look attractive and lean become lost buried under this avalanche of fat.

This fat invades every part of our frame, killing all the attractive features of our facade.

This accumulation of fat makes our appearance grotesque and frankly ludicrous.

People look at us differently, in an era when most of us want to become fit, suitable and attractive.

One of the damages caused by this mountain of fat, is to sap our energy; we lose our strength and become feeble.

We become unable to achieve certain chores we used to complete with ease.

Some of us become so desperate that we start envisioning weight reduction surgery.

Just reviewing these facts would make anyone mourn his youth forever, no matter the benefits that could also be part of aging.

H.C.B

06-13-15

Chapter 6: Sleep and Sleep Related Conditions

_The profound analogy
between Sleep and Death

_The marvels of Sleep Study
and Sleep Pharmacology

_The wonders of Sleep Study

_Sleep Disorders DSM-5 Version

The Profound analogy
between Sleep and Death

There has always been an analogy between Sleep and Death.

There is a certain twin-ship between the two situations.

Death is usually considered, as an eternal rest while Sleep is an intermittent one, which is designed to replenish people's energy allowing them to go on with living.

Death is a complete "shut down" of all bodily organs including the brain.

Sleep on the other hand is a "slow down" of all metabolic reactions in the body allowing it to revamp and refurbish all the components indispensable for survival.

We probably will never get to the bottom of this analysis, since realistically no one ever comes back from the dead.

Death that I like to describe; a stage I like to compare to an elegant sadistic and sophisticated lady.

The lady in black who is famous notorious for her impartiality.

She is renowned her sense of fairness.

She is also well known for preventing people from fleeing her world.

She usually does not give anybody a chance to describe her mysterious and frosty domain.

She has never as far as we know, allowed or granted anybody the privilege of evading her frigid world; whether black, white or yellow.

Once one is admitted there, one should reside at this location for eternity.

However when one falls asleep, he or she should not stay asleep forever unless one slip into a comatose state.

Even in this eventuality some subjects come back from a coma after staying in this state for days, months or even years.

It seems like the matter of "Death versus Sleep" is, simply put whether one can or can't come back from these lethargic states.

In reality it is more complicated than that. After death the body decomposes and later changes completely to become dust. While there usually is no such thing when one falls asleep since the body maintains its integrity.

In addition there is the spiritual aspect that comes in line; the spirit is reportedly lifted from the body after death while after having some resting sleep, one's spirit does not usually go anywhere.

H.C.B

08-17-15

The marvels of sleep study and sleep Pharmacology.

Sleep study and Sleep pharmacology are awesome and fascinating when you consider some of the most recent discoveries in the field.

The Homeostasis, which is a state of equilibrium of sleep, includes a need to restore energy that increases throughout the day until at some point certain adenosine related processes, trigger a need to sleep.

It is reported that in sleep-deprived individuals, the brain maximizes sleep functions and recovery time by increasing slow wave sleep activity; that seems to make sense, since slow wave sleep is equivalent to deep sleep.

In "circadian rhythms", characterized by events occurring every twenty-four hours creating therefore a cycle of biological activities or functions, like sleep time and wake time.

It is important to know that body temperature usually decreases in the afternoon, triggering a desire to nap. Sleep and wake time are gated by a circadian clock. An amazing finding is the discovery that the most intense need for sleep coincides with the lowest body temperature occurring around 3-4 am in Human Beings.

It is also believed that body temperature also decreases in the afternoon thus triggering a desire to nap. In human sleep-wake cycle, sleep is easiest during nighttime.

Sleep deprivation could affect different areas of the brain such as the "inferior parietal cortex" where there is a hypo metabolic state manifested by an inability to pay attention.

The "prefrontal cortex" could also be affected causing some impaired decision-making. Some people suffer from some mood deregulation and have difficulties interacting with each other, when the "thalamus" is involved.

According to some recently done researches, sleep restriction causes level of norepinephrine to rise at significant rate throughout the day.

It has also been discovered that brief naps of approximately 8 minutes in am and 11 minutes in the afternoon counterbalance all these hormonal changes.

People, who suffer from insomnia, usually have an inability to shut down their "reticular activating system" (RAS) at night. It is thought that some conditions like "restless leg syndrome" may be partly caused by a dopamine deficiency.

According to some recently done studies, some chemical compounds such as: "adenosine", "y-aminobutyric acid", "galanin", "melatonin", are considered "promoters of sleep". While some others like: "histamine", "serotonin", "norepinephrine", "orexin" (hypocretin) are considered "promoters of wakefulness".

Narcolepsy is viewed as a genetically predisposed autoimmune response to benign infections resulting in the destruction of "orexin" producing cell in the "perifornical area of the hypothalamus". The loss of "orexin" subsequently cause the patient to lose control of the transition from wakefulness to sleep and fall asleep abruptly while he is still in rapid eye movement (REM) state. The patient remains in REM after awakening and have a temporary paralysis.

The discovery of "orexin", an awakening compound gives birth to a new generation of sleep medications: "the orexin receptor antagonist" that are sleep-promoting agent still being studied.

This new group of sleep inducing medications will probably soon increase our biological arsenal against insomnia. In addition to the benzodiazepines like "temazepan" and "lorazepam" that are agonist at the y-aminobutyric receptors, the non-benzo diazepines like "zolpidem" (ambien), "zapleton" (sonata), "Zoplicone" (lunesta) are partial agonists at the same receptors. There is also a group of "off label medications" including: Seroquel, trazodone that are used frequently. Some "tricyclic antidepressant": doxepin, Elavil; some antihistamine like "hydroxyzine pamoate" (vistaril), hydroxyzine (Atarax) have short acting benefits since they don't last for more than 4 days.

Sedating antidepressant like mirtazapine (remeron) not only help with sleep and depression but also with anxiety.

In individuals with PTSD, who have nightmares as a prominent symptom a medication like (prazosin) improve these patients' sleep by minimizing, diminishing their nightmares.

Melatonin a more natural compound does not usually help with sleep onset, it may possibly helps with maintenance.

However the "Melatonin receptor Agonist" has affinity for melatonin receptors Mt1 and Mt2, located at the "suprachiasmatic nucleus" of the brain.

In this group, there are medications like "ramelteon" (rozerem) and "tasimelteon" (hetlioz); a cluster that is progressively growing, since these researchers are learning about the brain exponentially every single day.

H.C.B

06-03-15

The Wonders of Sleep Study

As a Physician, having to treat a condition such as "Insomnia" can be very challenging.

There are so many potential etiologies for this condition that prevent people from having the restoring ability of getting their energy back.

In order to be able to treat insomnia, one has to be able to pinpoint the cause of it.

The causes are multiple, sometime thorny, problematic.

Just doing certain activities, such as eating or watching TV in our bed, or even going to bed at different time every single day, can trigger the disorder.

They then talk about having bad sleep hygiene that have to be remedied, that must be corrected in order to have some sound sleep and be able to function.

Using certain substances like "Caffeine" can be implicated.

"Caffeinated beverages" such as: Tea, Coffee, Soft Drink, Chocolate can be a factor, mostly when one goes to bed right after drinking them.

In order to prevent that, one should avoid the consumption of these beverages right before going to bed.

It probably should be fine if we keep a window of approximately eight hours, which is roughly the equivalent of the half-life of caffeine.

A large number of mental and physical illnesses can be a cause for insomnia.

Among the mental illnesses, Anxiety Disorders, Mood Disorders including unipolar and bipolar depression, some Psychotic Disorders should also be on the list because of the fact the sufferer could be hearing voices that prevent him/her from sleeping. Sometime the psychotic subject could be so paranoid that he will keep himself awake in order to make sure he is not subjected to any assaults that could jeopardize his physical integrity.

Physical Disorders such as Asthma, Heart Failure, COPD (Chronic Obstructive Pulmonary Disease), and some Chronic Pain Syndrome can all keep the sufferer awake because of the discomfort and the pain associated with these illnesses.

Going back to caffeine, another compound that is also part of the group of stimulants such as Cocaine, Amphetamine, and Methamphetamine that have an effect similar to Caffeine as far as being a cause for insomnia.

Alcohol is another substance that can have a protracted effect, inducing therefore an insomnia, which could last long after the individual stop drinking.

Some other conditions are simply almost impossible to diagnose as a cause of insomnia unless one utilizes "Sleep Study", a procedure that has done wonders in its ability to pinpoint insomnia.

Therefore making a visit to the "Sleep Lab" can help diagnose some lethal conditions such as "Sleep Apnea" and some others like "Restless Leg Syndrome", when we do not have a clue about what cause the insomnia and have been doing some "gun shot therapy" in an attempt to treat it.

In order to save the day "Sleep Studies" can do wonders in these circumstances, marveling the science behind this intervention.

H.C.B

09-05-15

Sleep Disorders as per the DSM-5 Version

The new DSM encompasses ten categories of sleep disorders or sleep-wake disorders. They are listed as followed: The Insomnia Disorders, Hyper somnolence Disorders, Narcolepsy, Breathing Related Sleep Disorders, Circadian Rhythm Sleep-Wake Disorders, (NREM) Non Rapid Eye Movements Sleep arousal Disorders, Nightmares Disorders, (REM) Rapid Eye Movements Sleep Behavior Disorders, Restless Legs Syndrome and Substances/ Medications induced Sleep Disorders.

The individuals suffering from these disorders usually present with sleep/wake complaints of dissatisfaction regarding the quality, timing and amount of their sleep. These disorders habitually result in daytime distress and impairments, which are the core features, shared by all of these sleep disorders.

It is emphasized that the DSM-5 Sleep Disorder Nosology uses a simple clinically useful approach while reflecting at the same time on some scientific advances in epidemiology, genetics and pathophysiologic assessment and intervention researches.

The new DSM uses a lumping approach for the Insomnia Disorders whereas in Narcolepsy a splitting approach has been taken reflecting the availability of validators derived from epidemiological, neurological and interventions research.

Sleep Disorders are often comorbid to some other Mental Disorders like Depression, Anxiety and cognitive changes that must be addressed in their treatment. Another risk is that persistence of insomnia and excessive sleepiness are causes for the development of subsequent mental illnesses and substance use disorders.

As a rule Sleep Disorder furnishes a clinically useful indicator of Medical and Neurological conditions that often coexist with Depression and other Mental Disorders.

Among these, it is worth mentioning Breathing Related Sleep Disorders, Disorders of the heart and lung (CHF "Congestive Heart Failure", COPD "Chronic Obstructive Pulmonary Disease"), some Neurodegenerative Disorder (Alzheimer's), Disorders of the Musculo-Skeletal System (Osteoarthitis). These Disorders not only disrupt sleep, they may also worsened during sleep (prolonged apnea with cardiac arrhythmia during REM Sleep; confusional arousals in patients with demented illnesses, seizure in patients with complex partial seizure.

"REM Sleep Behavioral Disorders" is often an early indicator of "neurodegeneratives disorders" (alpha sinucleinoopathies) like Parkinson Disease.

The Classification of Sleep Disorders in the DSM-5 can be understood in the context of lumping versus splitting. DSM-5 represents an effort to simplify the Sleep-Wake Disorders classifications. The use of Biological validators in DSM-5 is now embodied in the classifications of sleep-wake disorders particularly for conditions like "Narcolepsy", "Breathing Related Sleep Disorders" for which formal sleep studies (Polysomnography) are indicated; "Restless Legs Syndrome" which can be associated with periodic limbs movement during sleep is detectable as well by this screening method.

H.C.B

01-06-15

Chapter 7:
Culture and Cultural Matter

_The possession phenomenon
in the Voodoo Religion

_Haitian Mentality

_The powerful impact of culture
in people's life style

_Culture and Mental Health Diagnosis

The possession phenomenon in the voodoo religion

The possession phenomenon is probably one of the most puzzling features of the voodoo religion.

Even though it seems quite common in some other religions, it appears more striking and colorful when it relates to the voodoo religion. There are some physical and behavioral clues that could be a harbinger of this phenomenon. The precursors of this process could by example be reflected on the subject's facial expression, his inability to stand up still, his sudden drop to the ground and his subsequently rolling his eyes while screaming, groaning and moaning.

When the possessed is being asked to describe what has happened to him?

He said that, out of the blue he had the feeling that he is going to pass out.

He does not feel stable on his gait, which becomes wobbling, and it is like he is about to lose his balance.

He also describes the feeling of having an external force taking over his body.

He has the feeling that a weight is pressuring the back of his neck.

He perceives his hand as becoming so heavy, that he has the weird feeling of wearing some metallic gloves.

The possessed gradually reaches a point where he has more and more difficulties perceiving, defining himself as a person.

In other word, he feels spaced out.

His last perceived feeling is that he is about to fall and people around him attempt to support him in order to prevent his fall.

Then it is total black out, a complete obscurity; he does not have any more thoughts, he does not have any more feelings and he is unable to perceive his behavior.

There is a total take over of his being and he becomes inexistent, as if he was virtually dead.

He later wakes up sitting in a chair where he is being placed, wondering about what has happened to him.

At this particular time the post possession period, he reports feeling amazingly good, relaxed and serene.

Like somebody who had a seizure episode, he has no recollection of the event.

The possessed is designated in the voodoo world, as being the horse of the voodoo divinity possessing him.

On some occasion the possession crisis could be ferocious, mostly when the possessed has not yet been tamed.

When entirely tamed, he fully identifies himself with the voodoo divinity, mimicking his appearance and his behavior.

The voodoo divinity "Legba" comes across as an elderly man ambulating with a cane.

"Erzulie" for her part usually presents herself as a feisty, sophisticated, elegant and coquette woman asking traditionally for perfume.

"Damballah" is like a snake moving on the ground while ingurgitating or demanding to ingurgitate an egg.

"Hogou" is the fierce warrior with a cigar and a machete.

"Zaca" is a peasant wearing a hat and a bag across his chest.

These possessed voodoo practitioners have usually a lot of power. They could be very strong and incredibly resistant.

They can spend hours dancing without any sign of fatigue. They could move some heavy object they normally would have been unable to move, when they are back to their normal state.

They are often insensitive to fire and could be sometime observed devouring pieces of glittering wood, just like they would do for pieces of bread.

These possessed individuals could have "glossolalia" and become able to speak any language. They can imitate the way, in other word the "speaking habit" of the "voodoo divinity" or "Loa". This is what explains that their voice could sometimes have a nasal tone just like the divinity himself.

In order to conclude the description of this fascinating phenomenon, representing the "scene of possession" in the voodoo religion; an experience that had also happened in some other religions in a somewhat similar but less colorful fashion; we can simply state that regardless of the diversity of opinions on the subject, the fact is for the possessed voodoo practitioner who belongs to the voodoo cult, the "possession phenomenon" is truly a take over of a human being by some external, enigmatic and powerful force.

H.C.B
06-13-15

Haitian Mentality

In my country, the prime factor is money.

This sounds like a universal law, since everywhere in the world money is the primary factor for most people.

Money seems to be "the man", money seems to be a magical entity because of its tremendous power over everything, or what seems to be everything or most things.

However, when we avoid having a tunnel vision.

When we try to be more analytic, more realistic, more open minded, we probably could ask ourselves, is it really the case?

Is money really "the man"?

Some folks, who like to think that they are wise and fully mature state: "Money does not make you a man, men are capable of manufacturing money, make money from their employment, but you need more than money in or der to be an accomplished man".

They also could be very rich, mighty rich but their wealth their fortune does not make them perfect.

People probably need more than money in order to be perfect if they will ever be perfect, I strongly believe no one is perfect since perfection is not part of our world.

All of these ethical considerations, are to address the fact that in Haiti as in many other countries, a lot families give their daughters in order for them to marry a rich man regardless of their daughter's feelings; ignoring the fact that they probably are not in love with their future husbands and they more likely never will be. But it does not matter as long as "Mom and Dad" are happy once their financial problems are resolved. Their progenitors do not need to be overly sentimental since they will eventually get used to their husband and ultimately they will end up at least "liking" him.

However it is not always that simple and a lot of parents end up ruining the life of their children; who being unhappy do not usually go far with their marriage. They end up in a disaster with all kinds of ugliness associated with it. They end up dealing with domestic abuse, marital infidelities; and even some members of the third generation could be touched. In other word their grand children could be affected as well because of the psychological debacle that often becomes part of the general picture.

We can't therefore ignore the moral aspect surging with these practices, when the family of the bride is covered with shame because of their involvement in this tradition and their causing so many victims.

Since definitely, placing money over your family, clearly indicates how immoral and greedy some parents could be.

Parents should not put their children through this ordeal, they should instead let them freely pick their mate and later take full responsibility for their pick, if it turns out to be a miscue they should be the one to endure the consequences and deal with it.

In other word let them pick their poison, if in fact it turns out to be a poison. If they truly pickup a poison, you can bet they will be the first to realize it and they will have to absorb all the impacts, all the blames connected to their mistakes. I have learned over the years that there is always a price to pay for every mistake we make in life.

H.C.B

05-30-15

The Powerful impact of culture on people's life style

People all over the world come from different ethnic groups different geographic areas and they do have different customs.

As such they do have different opinions, different approaches to resolve crisis or conflicts.

Every ethnic group from different geographic area does things its own specific unique way, and has its own style.

When different ethnic groups from different geographic regions observe each other, what they usually perceive is another group of individuals who are doing things differently, resolving matters in an alternative way.

As a result of what they have perceived or seen, they do have a natural tendency to deem what is different from their usual habitual way, as odds, bizarre, abnormal.

In reality there is nothing abnormal about it, being different does not mean being abnormal, or odd. Having different separate alternative beliefs does not make any one insane.

It is not a barometer to assess insanity; it is not a tool to evaluate craziness, it is not an instrument to determine whether someone is berserk.

For some group the number thirteen by example means that bad, evil, malefic predictions are on the horizon

It reveals an emblem that mayhem is taking over one's life; it is an indication that havoc is on the way.

For another cluster of individuals, seeing a black cat might predict the arrival of an enigmatic supernatural or superstitious phenomenon.

Some other factions consider normal to hear the voice of a relative right after his or her death.

While another group may view hearing the voices of a deceased relative, as having auditory hallucinations.

I say all of this to imply that people's culture naturally has a profound impact on their life style regardless of what some pundits may think.

This is part of the way this particular ethnicity or group of individuals envision matters according to the backgrounds of their ancestors.

H.C.B

08-22-15

Culture and mental Health Diagnosis

The patient's cultural background is possibly one of the most common reasons why they are wrongfully diagnosed as having a mental health condition.

As an example, someone who claims to be hearing voices when there is nobody around is often diagnosed as having a psychotic disorder.

However if this person comes from an area where it is considered normal to hear the voice of a relative after his death. One can't diagnose him as having a mental disorder since this is part of his cultural background.

In some culture people think the boogeyman could be after them in order to cause harm to them. Such belief may be considered delusional for someone coming from a western country, but it is not, it is just cultural part of the general belief of this particular faction of characters.

We have heard of many culture-bound psychotic syndromes including: Amok, Koro, Piblokto and Wihtigo among others.

"Amok" is a word derived from the Malayan culture and means a "murderous frenzy". The amok syndrome consists of a sudden unprovoked outburst of wild rage, in which those affected run about madly and indiscriminately and maim any living souls on their path, whether human or animal.

This savage homicidal attack is often preceded by a period of preoccupation; brooding and mild depression when the person feels exhausted.

He/she has no memory of the attack and often commits suicide subsequently. A cultural belief in magical possession by demons and evil spirits may be another factor contributing to the development of the amok syndrome.

"Koro" is characterized by the fact a patient has the delusional belief his penis is shrinking and may disappear into his abdomen causing his death as a result. The "Koro syndrome" occurs among people in South Asia and in some area of china where it is known as "suk-yeong". In the women equivalent of the disorder the woman complains of a shrinkage of the of the vulva, the labia and the breasts.

"Piblokto", another culturally bound psychotic syndrome usually occurs among the "Inuit". Also called arctic hysteria, it is characterized by attacks lasting from one to two hours during which affected people who are usually women begin to scream and tear off and destroy their clothing. While imitating the cry of an animal, usually a bird; affected people may throw themselves in the snow or run wildly on ice.

"Wihtigo" or "Windigo" another component of this group of culturally related psychosis, is a psychiatric disorder confined to the Cree, Ojibwa and Salteaux of North America. Affected people believe that they have been transformed into a "wihtigo" or a "giant monster" that easts human flesh. During a period of starvation, they may feel and express a craving for human flesh.

In some Caribbean cultures, some individuals could be hit by a curse or some sort of maleficent deed that makes them appeared as if they were dead. This death seems so amazingly and incredibly real, that the subject relatives start desperately to scream and cry for their lost while following the funeral procession leading to their being laid to rest. The night following the funeral, they hear the deceased yell from their being mistreated by their malefactors ordering them to utter that they are passing by. This is what the "Zombification" or "Zombie Phenomenon" is all about in certain cultures!

In this particular scenario, people from some western countries would consider them delusional and think they do have a delusional disorder.

Anything, that is part of anybody's culture, cannot be judged or perceived as a delusion. That is the reason we should be very careful as mental health professionals about labeling people as having a mental disorder when some of their beliefs are part of their cultural background.

H.C.B

08-23-15

Chapter 8:
Developmental Matter

_Is Adolescence and Getting Berserk synonymous?

Is Adolescence and getting berserk synonymous?

According to a review done by a prominent paper, Adolescence is perceived as being synonymous with risk taking, emotional upheaval and erratic behavior.

This outlandish, off-the-wall behavior is usually associated with the hormonal explosion happening during this milestone.

At this stage of their life, they usually face a number of challenges.

This angst that comes naturally with this special landmark, has many explanations.

The Adolescent longs for being independent to discover, he is still strongly dependent from his progenitors.

He is wrestling with these issues, while he is still trying to overcome an identity crisis.

Some people in the scientific world believe the adolescent is subjected to an abrupt twist in the development of his brain.

It is thought that the "Amygdala" which is the brain circuit for processing fear and emotion, is precocious and develops way ahead of the "Pre Frontal Cortex", the center for reasoning and executive control. This viewpoint associates the adolescent's behavior to the anatomic and physiologic aspect of his brain.

As stated earlier this reasoning focuses more on the anatomical and physiological aspect of the adolescent's brain, rather than the psychological or the psychodynamic one.

The Adolescent brain is perceived as wired with an enhanced capacity for fear and anxiety, and is considered underdeveloped for reasoning and self-composure.

The ability for the adolescent to be novelty's seeking and risk taker and be at the same time so susceptible to bouts of anxiety seems paradoxical.

However the explanation given by the author of this article is again mostly anatomical and physiological. The author believes, the "Brain Reward Center" just like its "Fear Circuit", matures earlier than the "Prefrontal Cortex". Therefore this is the "Rewards Center" with its overflow of "Dopamine" the "hedonic biogenic amine" neurotransmitter that drives most of the adolescent risky behavior.

This is also why Adolescents are so prone to injury and trauma.

Indeed, according to some statistics the top three killers of teenagers are: Accidents, Homicides and Suicides. It seems like the development of the brain has a huge impact on how, we human beings particularly during the phase of adolescence think about anxiety, and how we treat it.

It suggests that anxious adolescents may not be very responsive to psychotherapy attempting to teach them to be unafraid like CBT (Cognitive Behavior Therapy).

The rising use of stimulants in young people worsen anxiety, and makes it harder for Teenagers to do what they were developmentally suppose to do, learn to be unafraid when it is appropriate to do so.

Adolescents learn to modulate their fear as their "prefrontal cortex" matures in "young adulthood" when they become 25 years old approximately.

The prevalence of "anxiety disorders" reflects this developmental dysfunction in the brain. That is probably why up to 20% of Adolescents in the US experience a diagnosable anxiety disorder like GAD (General Anxiety Disorder), Panic Disorder, resulting from a mix of genetic factors, physiological and environmental influences. The "Amygdala" is critical in evaluating fear. It is connected to the "Prefrontal Cortex" and is alerting us about danger even before we have time to think about it.

The "Amygdala" usually sends instantaneous fear signals, and the "Prefrontal Cortex" accepts or rejects them based on merit.

It is important to know that, contrarily to the "Amygdala", the "Prefrontal Cortex" is the last brain region to mature; that is why Adolescents have far less ability to modulate emotion.

All this ebullition, this volcanic eruption that happen during this period is not due to the stage itself, but rather to a combination of factors including the delay, the time taken by the "Prefrontal Cortex" to finally mature, along with the early development of the "Amygdala" and the "Reward Center" of the brain, in addition to the "Hormonal Flooding" that occur during this milestone.

H.C.B

02-21-15

Chapter 9:
Mind over Matter

_The Power of the Mind and the Survival Instinct

The Power of the mind and the Survival Instinct

We will never stop mentioning, the powerful ability of our mind, since it has outlasted our body in so many circumstances.

When we feel weak and unable to tackle an assignment, we consciously or unconsciously call our mind to the rescue.

Most of us instinctively know the unlimited potential of our mind.

We often talk about being "emotionally prepared" every single time the power of our brain bails us out.

When we are agonizing, when we feel seriously challenged, we instinctively switch into a pilot mode, allowing us to tackle via "our soul" our "mighty mind", the completion of the objective in line.

We have realized in so many occasions, time and time again, how being backed up by the strength of "our spirit" is indispensable to us.

We have come to use this tool naturally, every time we feel trapped; every time we feel tested, every stint we feel defied and anticipate the possibility of failure.

Rather than giving in, we feel that we have not use all our resources and still have a secret weapon that could lead us to victory and allow us to achieve our goal.

We still have this instrument that makes us feel good about ourselves.

Henry C. Barbot, M.D.

It is comforting to know that.

It is soothing to our confidence to know that we have this back up tool that will bail us out in any circumstance.

It is comforting to know that as long as our mind remains active and powerful, we should be able to use it over and over in order to overcome any challenge coming our way.

It is comforting to know that the power of our mind will help us consistently feed our survival instinct.

That is another perception that will always allow us to place it rightfully above any material entity

H.C.B
09-05-15

Chapter 10:
Biological Concepts

_Street Drugs and Medical Illnesses

_Scattered thoughts in Addiction Medicine

_The Hazards associated with
Psychotropic medications

_The Pluses and Minuses of the new DSM

_Pseudo Bulbar Affect and
Traumatic Brain Injury

_"Varenicline", another option for the
treatment of Alcohol Dependence

_The use of Gabapentin for
Alcohol Dependence

_Cannabis and abnormalities of
the "Nucleus Acumbens" and
the "Amygdala" in the Youth

_Prescribed Medications and False Positivity during Drug Testing

_Transcranial Near-Infrared Therapy, a new neuro-modulation technic for Depression

_The Biological aspect of Depression and Suicide

Street Drugs and Medical Illnesses

When we consider the medical complications of street drugs, the damages some of them could cause to our body, we often wonder why we are using them.

These drugs, whether they are considered legal or illegal do not discriminate, they all could systematically destroy our brain and our body.

We must first consider the so-called "legal drugs" which seem to be deadlier than the others that are so numerous in our streets and are considered illegal.

One of the members of this group "Caffeine" which is probably the most frequently consumed since a lot of us are using it.

Most of us indeed need some sort of booster, a lift to start our day.

Caffeine can be the ideal booster for some of us; this is probably why it is so popular and used so widely.

The Chemical in caffeine is a "Trimethylxanghine" acts as a "Phosphodiesterase inhibitor". This Trimethylxanthine" can cause: anxiety, tachycardia, and arrhythmias during intoxication. It can also cause another set of symptoms during withdrawal such as: headache, irritability, and inability to focus or stay awake.

Another member of the group of legal drugs, "tobacco or Nicotine" is considered the leading preventable cause of deaths. According to some statistics done in the late 90's, "Nicotine" can cause 438,000 deaths a year, 38,000 of them result from second hand smoking. It could be associated with a wide variety of pathologic processes, including low bone density, peptic ulcer disease, vascular disease (Intermittent claudication), low birth weight and "SIDS" (Sudden Infant Death Syndrome".

Nicotine is usually linked to a wide variety of neoplasms including: oral, laryngeal, pulmonary, esophageal, stomach, pancreatic, renal, bladder, cervix and acute myeloid leukemia. Moving to Alcohol, another member of the group of legal drugs. It is considered the third leading preventable cause of death. In addition to causing a wide variety of medical illnesses, it is reported that 40% of all crimes were committed under the influence of alcohol. Based on some statistics done in 1997, approximately 2/3 of victims of "intimate partners violence", known as "domestic violence", report alcohol as a causal factor. It is also believed that 72% of rapes in College campuses occur when the victims are intoxicated. Approximately one half of the cases of child abuse and neglect are thought to be associated with parental alcohol or drug abuse.

About 23% of death by suicide could be secondary to alcohol. Among the medical illnesses that are caused by alcohol, "Pancreatitis" is a common one.

Some liver ailments could be part of the damages triggered by alcohol on the human body. We can name in this group: "Alcohol Hepatitis" which is an inflammation of the liver occurring after a period of heavy drinking. "Hepatic Steatosis", a deposition of fat within the liver parenchyma another casualty of alcohol on the liver. At a more advanced phase, "cirrhosis" which includes "fibrosis", "portal hypertension" with "esophageal varicose", "ascites", "coagulopathies" and "hepatocellular carcinomas".

"Gastritis" an inflammation of the gastric mucosa, another casualty caused by alcohol.

In the pregnant women, one of the complications of alcohol dependence is: "Fetal Alcohol Syndrome".

A potentially lethal withdrawal syndrome: "Delirium Tremens" or "DT" could occur as well.

A series of malignancies as mentioned earlier could be part of the bleak picture of damages caused by alcohol. The followings are the most notorious: Cancer of the throat, the esophagus, the mouth, the liver, the prostate and the breast in women.

Switching to the "Inhalants" such as: "Nitrous Oxides", "Nitrites", among others. These compounds can cause vasodilation, tachycardia and smooth muscles relaxation. Some others like "Model Glue", "Toluene", "Butane', "spot removers", "Trichloroethylene", "correction fluid". All these products can cause cardiac arrhythmias, the so-called "Sudden Sniffing Death Syndrome" by interfering with oxygenation. In addition they can cause "peripheral neuropathy", "hepatic injury", "behavioral and cognitive impairments".

We will not overlook the performance enhancers such as: "The Anabolic Steroids" which can cause "atherogenic lipid changes" affecting the coronary vessels. They could be the cause for some "hepatic tumors", "anemia and aggression". "Rhoid Rage" is a well-known bout of aggression often caused by the "anabolic steroid".

"Growth Hormone" is also part of the performance enhancers possibly causing "edema and elevated glucose".

Finally "Erythropoietin" which is also part of this group can cause "Hyperviscosity" and "Polycytemia Vera".

Pursuing our exploration of these street drugs, another group, the "Cannabinoids", recently amended into legal drugs by some "States of the Union" probably will soon be part of the group of legal drugs. Among the "Cannabinoids": "Marijuana", "Hashish",

"Dronabinol (Marinol)", "Nabilone (Cesamet)" have a wide range of side effects such as: "tachycardia", "dizziness", "drowsiness", "dysphoria", and "visual hallucinations". The spraying of "Paraquat" an "anticannabis herbicide" could cause "acute pulmonary toxicity with cough". These compounds can also cause accelerated "hippocampal neuronal loss" with increased work related injuries and absenteeism. In the Newborn the so-called innocent victims, there are some findings in children's testing including: "deficit in problems solving skills" and "memory" as well as some "deficit in the ability to focus".

Considering "The Stimulants" such as "Amphetamines", "Methamphetamine (Crystal Meth, Ice)", "Methylphenidate", they usually impact the human body by causing some "cardio-vascular complications" related to their "alpha and beta-adrenergic agonist properties". They also cause some "Neuro-Behavioral" complications related to their ability to release dopamine at the nerve terminal and the synapse. "Stimulant Toxicity" can cause: "Hyperthermia", "tachycardia (Beta adrenergic)", "hypertension (Alpha and Beta)", "Myocardial Infarction", "seizure" "hemorrhagic stroke", resulting from the use of "Phenylpropanolamine" as an "appetite suppressant". In the long run these stimulants can also cause some cardiovascular toxicities such as "dilated cardiomyopathy" with "reduced ventricular function".

In addition to this litany of damages, one can register some "memory and learning impairment", some "anxiety", "paranoia" and other "psychotic symptoms". They can as well cause "formication (bug crawling feeling)", "bruxism (Grinding of the teeth)" and "anorexia". In the pregnant woman one can see a series of complications such as "premature delivery", "placenta abruption", "fetal growth retardation", "heart and brain abnormalities".

Continuing our coverage of the street drugs and their possible impact on human beings triggering so many medical complications; the next cluster to consider are the "Barbiturates".

As a group they can cause "depression of the respiratory drive", they are also likely to cause "tolerance and withdrawal syndrome".

Another faction that carries some analogy but is considered way safer than the Barbiturate, is the group constituted by the "Benzodiazepines". They can cause "anterograde amnesia", "confusion and somnolence" mostly in the elderly. They also can cause rebound "insomnia and withdrawal syndrome" and some fetal abnormalities in pregnancy such as "Floppy Infant syndrome" and "Oral cleft risks".

Switching to cocaine which should have been considered with the stimulants, its blocks the reuptake of norepinephrine in the preganglionic neuron. Therefore there is an excess signal to the postganglionic neurons. It causes some "cardiac complications" such as "increase in myocardial oxygen demand" and "vasoconstriction in the coronary artery". It produces "cocaine associated chest pain", "myocardial ischemia" and "myocardial infarction". It also causes "nasal septal perforation" and "Crack Lung" an acute hypersentivity reaction.

Cocaine can also induce "seizure", "intracranial hemorrhage", "hyperthermia" and rhabdomyolysis a muscle breakdown that often ends up in "renal failure". It crosses the placenta and "decreases uterine blood flow" producing "spontaneous abortion" and "placenta abruption". It increases the risk of "fetal growth retardation" with "premature delivery". In addition it increases the risk of "congenital malformation", "neonatal irritability", and long-term "neuro-behavioral problems (Crack Babies)".

Switching gear on "The Pschedelics" and "Anesthetics" or "Club Drugs" like: "LSD", "Mescaline", "Psilocybin", "Phencyclidine", "ketamine", "Ecstasy".

The user could have: "anxiety", "panic" provoking a "bad trip", "depression", "paranoia", "psychosis", "flashback".

"Phencyclidine" also name "PCP" or "Angel Dust" produces "hallucinations" by interacting with some neurotransmitters and creates "confusion and aggressive state".

"Ketamine" relates to PCP and can "increase the heart rate" and "the cardiac output" along with the "blood pressure" targeting the "cortex and the limbic system".

"Chemical Ecstasy" or (MDMA) "MethyleneDioxyMetamphetamine" increases serotonin and causes "hyperthermia", "seizure", "rhabdomyelosis", "fluid and electronic imbalance" and "hepatic injury".

"Liquid Ectasy" or (GHBUR) "GabaHydroybutiric", a date rape drug now approved for narcolepsy. This drug causes "confusion", "hallucinosis", "coma", "respiratory depression", "fulminant hepatic failure' requiring liver transplant.

"Herbal Ecstasy": "Ephedra", "Mahuang", "ephedrine beta-agonist", "pseudoephrine", "phenyl propanolamine" can cause "myocardial infection", "strokes and sudden death".

Bearing in mind the Opiates, "Heroin" or "Diacetyl morphine". The Opiates targets receptors in the "locus cereleus". In toxic dose they can cause "respiratory depression", "coma", "reduced brainstem responsiveness to rising CO2" and "impaired pontine and medullary regulation" of breath rhythm. It causes dependence, "risk of pneumonia", "prolonged QT interval on the EKG" and "Constipation". During pregnancy it causes "Neonatal Abstinence Syndrome" with "low birth weight and Small head circumference".

Finally the "Dissolving Agents" or contaminants like: "sugar, flour, quinine, starch, talc", can lodge in the alveolar capillaries and develop "talc granuloma", a condition triggered by the dissolving agents that could be worse that the drugs themselves.

H.C.B

05-04-15

Scattered thoughts in Addiction Medicine

I often have some scattered thoughts concerning the treatment approaches to the addiction to most common street drugs including: Cocaine, Phencyclidine, Cannabis, Alcohol, Opiates as well as some designer drugs.

It is important to emphasize that, in order to concoct a treatment for the intoxication or withdrawal to most street-drugs, one must know the half-life of the drug, that is the usual time it stays in our system.

Starting with "Alcohol", it stays in the human body up to 24 hours and therefore can be detected in the urine, up to 24 hours after a drink.

We also know that one serving of alcohol is fully absorbed one half to two hours after intake. The body can metabolize one quart of an ounce of alcohol per hour; however many factors have to be considered including: the size and weight of the person, the metabolic rate, the food intake and the type of beverage consumed.

"Alcohol" is generally absorbed relatively quickly but it is metabolized much more slowly.

It is believed that a 150lbs individual adds about 0.02%of alcohol per hour to his BAC (Blood Alcohol Concentration), he however removes 0.01% from its total blood alcohol concentration. That is the reason why the blood alcohol concentration is built steadily during a drinking session.

A BAC "Blood Alcohol Concentration" of alcohol of 0.100 could be detected up to 8 hours after achieving this level because of the slow removal of alcohol in the blood as described previously.

Moving to "Cocaine", it peaks in the blood in half an hour. In general cocaine and its metabolites can be detected in the body up to 2-4 days after use.

When snorting the level of cocaine peaks in half an hour. Oral administration of cocaine peaks in two hours. Smoking crack cocaine peaks in 45 minutes. The apparent half-life of cocaine is very short: two hours. However with chronic use, cocaine and its metabolites stay longer in the body.

The main metabolite of cocaine: "Benzoylecgonine" can be detected in the urine up to 2-4 days for a "sporadic users"; but it could stay as long as twelve days for a "chronic users".

For intra venous users, the duration is 1.5 day, but the drug could stay up to a week and as long as 3 weeks in some unusual circumstances

Switching to "Cannabis", which usually stays in the blood for weeks. It can be detected in the blood after a few hours since it is important to know that urine test only shows recent use of THC.

However some THC metabolites have a long half-life about 20 hours, therefore urine test for Cannabis can also detect the drug up to 13 days after use. "Regular smokers" have tested positive for the drugs up to 45 days after use, while "heavy smokers" could stay positive up to a whooping 90 days.

It is also important to know that "Ibuprofen" could cause cannabis to become falsely positive.

Focusing on "Phencyclidine" (PCP), this compound stays in the blood for approximately 7-11 hours. However because of its being fat soluble, it could be detected in the urine up to 48 hours or longer.

Bearing in mind the "Opioids", "Heroin" has a half- life of only 3-8 minutes. It is therefore completely out of the body in a couple of days even in heavy users. This is a "schedule I control substance", that can't be obtained by a Dr.'s prescription. It is metabolized into "morphine" by the human body and "morphine itself has a half-live of 3-6 hours". "Heroin" stays in the blood for 1 day and in the urine for 1- 2days but it usually stays in the "patient's hair for up to 90 days".

Going back to "Cocaine", the pharmacological or biological treatment of cocaine addiction has different approaches including: "Immune therapy" or "cocaine vaccination", which provides antibody to cocaine, preventing the drug from reaching the CNS (Central Nervous System) "Xenova Vaccine 2,000 Mcg".

The "Endogenous Cannabinoid System", has been implicated in Cocaine addiction. "CB1 receptor agonist/ inverse agonist" diminishes acquisition and maintenance of intravenous cocaine. That is probably why "Rimonabant" reduces cue and drug-primed which conditioned cocaine relapse in animals.

The use of CB1 Antagonists/inverse agonists in cocaine use disorder, is an area for further inquiry.

The "Glutamatergic Agents" such as "Modafinil", a wake-promoting agent used to treat narcolepsy has been used in cocaine addiction as well. One of the pharmacologic properties of this medication is to increase extracellular glutamate level, restoring the tone of the "presynaptic metabotropic glutamate receptors (mGluR2/3)" and decreasing glutamate surge associated with drug reinstatement. "Modafinil" seems to be a good treatment for prolonged abstinence from cocaine when compared to placebo.

"Cocaine addiction" is associated with, a large presynaptic release of glutamate in projection from The "PFC (Pre-frontal Cortex)" to the "NA (Nucleus Acumbens)", an "Up-regulation of post-synaptic

AMPA receptors", and a "Down-regulation in the pre-synaptic metabotropic glutamate receptors (mGluR2/3)".

Another agent used in cocaine addiction is "N-acetylcystein" which is a "cysteine glutamate exchanger" that restores the extra cellular level of glutamate, which from its part may restore inhibitory tone by "activating mGluR2/3 receptors" that prevents "synaptic glutamate release associated with drug-seeking behavior".

This has been shown to reduce cocaine craving in a trial of cocaine dependents patients. In addition specific "mGluR2/3 agonists" have been associated with "diminished cocaine seeking behavior in animals".

"Serotonergic Agents": Since Cocaine inhibits the serotonin transporter (SAT) and has a high affinity for the "5HT3 receptor as an agonist". The "SSRI" have no impact whatsoever in cocaine addiction. However a "5HT3 antagonist" like "Ondansetron" has shown some efficacy in reducing cocaine self-administration in laboratory animals. Some studies in cocaine dependent patients found a reduction in cocaine use by using this compound.

"Gaba-ergic Agents" such as: "Baclofen", "Tiagabine", "Vigabatrin", "Topiramate", "Valproic acid" and "Vigabatrin" "Sabril" (Gamma-vinyl-Gaba), an irreversible inhibitor of GABA has been shown to have anti-addictive properties for people who are addicted to cocaine."Topiramate" (enhanced GABAergic activity and has an "antagonist property" at the "AMPA and Kainite glutamate receptors" in a 13 weeks double blind/placebo controlled trial of at least 40 cocaine addicts. Its used at a dose of 200mg/day, was clearly superior to placebo in achieving and maintaining abstinence from cocaine (59% vs. 26%).

"Topiramate" therefore has promising result in "cocaine addiction" and as a relapse prevention tool in the treatment for "Alcohol Dependence".

It probably could become an agent that can reduce both alcohol and Cocaine in patients with co-occurring "substance used disorders" (SUDs)

"Valproic acid", which increases the synthesis of GABA and potentiates its presynaptic release and postsynaptic response, has been associated with decreased cocaine used.

Some "Aversive Conditioning" could be successful as well. There is a high co-occurrence of alcohol dependence in cocaine dependent patients up to 85%. A reduction in alcohol consumption as part of the (DER) "Disulfiram Ethanol Reaction" would also indirectly lead to a reduction of cocaine consumption. In fact this so called "aversive conditioning" can possibly lead to a reduction of both alcohol and cocaine when compared to placebo.

Some evidence-based studies also emphasized that "Disulfiram" even work better in the cocaine dependent patient, who does not drink. The way this drug works for cocaine dependent patients is based on its ability to inhibit "Dopamine Beta Hydroxylase" or (DBH), the "enzyme that converts dopamine to norepinephrine" therefore leading to a "built-up of dopamine", which works as "dopamine agonist" subsequently decreasing the need for cocaine; since cocaine ultimately increases the level of dopamine in some hedonic areas of the brain.

Considering the same rational described previously some "Dopamine enhancing agents" such as "Amantadine" has shown some promise in treating patient with cocaine dependence.

Another strategy is to use a "long acting dopamine agonist" like "amphetamine" to decrease the craving for cocaine, which is a "short acting dopamine agonist". This method is "similar to the use of methadone" to "decrease the craving triggered by heroin". In a way this method is like treating an addictive disorder by substituting it with another one.

Moving on to target opioid addiction the "Iboga Alkaloids" which have a complicated set of receptors targeting serotonin along with some "serotonin agonists" such as: 5HT2a, 5HT3; NMDA antagonism, "Opioid and Acetyl choline both "muscarinic agonist" and "nicotinic antagonist". These "iboga alkaloids" treat opioids withdrawal and are useful for relapse prevention.

They are not used in the US because of their potential for "neurotoxicity" and "cardio toxicity".

They also talk about "CRF-antagonists" and "naltrexone maintenance" ("naltrexone" and "vivitrol") for relapse prevention in opiate addicts

"Buprenorphine Maintenance", that is using "buprenorphine a partial mu agonist", with a maximal dose "equivalent to 70 mg of methadone" (Optimal dose of methadone "80 mg -120 mg"). "Depot Buprenorphine" is actively being studied to treat opiate addiction.

At this moment "8 mg of buprenorphine sublingual" demonstrated better treatment retention and lower opiate use when compare to "20 mg of methadone".

"Buprenorphine", being "a partial mu agonist" can precipitate withdrawal on a patient who is on a "full mu agonist".

In order to start working with a patient who is on a full mu agonist, the "dose of buprenorphine" must be "equivalent to 30-40 mg of methadone".

Induction must be done over a "4 day period" with a typical "initial dose of 4 mg sublingual" once the patient is in active withdrawal. After 1- 2hours, "if the patient is still in withdrawal a second dose of 4 mg is given", if necessary a third dose is given several hours later if needed with a "maximum of 12mg" on the first day.

Subsequently on day two "additional doses of 4mg every 2 hours" up to a "maximum of 8mg for the day", the typical "maintenance dose is 16-24 mg with a ceiling of 32mg/day".

In order to avoid abuse or diversion with buprenorphine, it is usually developed in a "combination form with naltrexone (suboxone)", vs the "monoform of buprenorphine alone ("subutex")".

When "suboxone" is taken in a sublingually, the "naloxone component has a poor bioavailability and is mostly inactive". However when liquefied and taken parentally, "the naloxone constituent become active and can induce opiate withdrawal".

"Buprenorphine" is a long acting up to "48 hours partial mu-opioid agonist and kappa antagonist" in which its "high affinity for the mu opioid receptor" causes it to act as a "functional antagonist", "blocking the effect of a pure mu agonist" except at a very high dose when the blockage could be overridden.

It is considered as a "schedule III drug" designed to treat opioid dependence.

Moving on to "Methadone Maintenance". This is the only treatment for opiate dependence that has clearly shown to diminish opiate use. Some of the benefits, "decreased morbidity and mortality" as well as "decreased transmissibility of viral infections (HIV, Hep C)" and "reduced criminal behavior". Although "30-40mg of methadone" suppresses most "craving and withdrawal symptoms", it is not sufficient in case of cross-tolerance, to block the reinforcing properties of high illicit opiate dose.

Some studies demonstrated that "high dose of methadone > 50mg /day was better than lower dose< 50 mg in reducing illicit opiated use" and the "optimal dose range of most methadone maintenance programs is between 80 mg-290 mg".

Methadone can be fatal in overdose with increased risk of "active liver disease". With concomitant use of alcohol, sedative- hypnotic (benzodiazepine, barbiturate, GHB) as well as some medications inhibiting the CYP3, which is the pathway, used by methadone for its metabolism; "It can have a synergistic effect and kill the respiratory drive". Another important issue is that "methadone accumulates erratically and can take over a week to reach steady state level" during the "induction phase". It is therefore strongly recommended that an "initial induction dose not to exceed 30 mg", and the "total dose for the first 24 hours not to exceed 40 mg" in order to avoid "overdose fatalities". "At dose above 120mg/day", methadone has been associated with possible "cardiac conduction problems (QT prolongation and the risk of Torsade de Pointes)". Unlike "heroin which has a half life of 1 hour", "Methadone has half life of 24-36 hours" and the "range is 13- 50 hours" and it can be dosed once daily. Side effects are "sweating, constipation, urinary retention and orgasmic dysfunction in men". It may also have cardio protective side effect by "reducing atherosclerotic plaque formation".

Switching to the pharmacological or biological treatment of "alcohol use disorder".

"Naltrexone" and "Acamprosate" may target different aspect of the relapse process. Some studies demonstrate that the combination of "acamprosate and naltrexone" was better than "acamprosate alone" but it was not better than "naltrexone alone".

"Disulfiram-naltxone" may be more effective in improving drinking outcome compare than "disulfiram alone"; and "disulfiram-acamprosate" may provide a higher degree of cumulative abstinence.

Some "Endo-cannabinoid Agents" may have a role in the treatment of Alcohol use disorders. Since some alcohol reinforcing properties are mediated by activating the "CB1 receptor", which is believed "to increase dopamine transmission" in the "mesolimbic circuit".

Some "CB1 antagonists/inverse agonists" were shown to "reduce alcohol intake" as well as "disrupt the relapse to alcohol seeking behaviors".

"Topiramate": "enhances Gaba-A activity, and diminishes glutamatergic transmission by antagonism at the Ampa and kainate glutamate receptors". "At a dose of 300 mg it is better than placebo in reducing heavy drinking and increasing the percentage of abstinent days".

"Baclofen": is useful not only to treat "alcohol withdrawal" but also "alcohol use". It helps in the prevention of relapse as well. The drug is a "selective metabotropic Gaba-B compound" that has shown some "promise in relapse prevention, abstinence maintenance and craving".

It seems to work by "selectively activating Gaba-B receptors on the VTA DA (Ventral Tegmental Area) DA", leading to a "reduction of dopamine release in the NA (Nucleus Acumbens)".

"Acamprosate's clinical efficacy" was well established in over a dozen studies in Europe where it consistently superior to placebo, in rates of total abstinence; it seems to benefit patient with greater severity of illness. It was approved as a "relapse prevention medication to treat alcohol dependence"

"Nalmefene": is similar to naltrexone and is a "non selective opiate antagonist" but one of "its advantage over naltrexone is its longer half life and lower prevalence of side effects mostly hepatotoxicity". It reduces voluntary alcohol consumption and relapse rates to heavy drinking similarly to naltrexone.

"Vivitrol": is a monthly injection formulation of naltrexone for the treatment of alcohol dependence. The justification for such a product is the poor adherence with the oral naltrexone, used to treat alcoholism. The lack of compliance is strongly correlated with highly relapse rate. Therefore "Vivitrol" "380mg im monthly injection over a 6 months period" significantly reduced median drinking day per month.

"Naltrexone": Some studies involving this product have shown a "reduction of the frequency of drinking, craving and relapse to heavy drinking" compared to placebo. However certain groups seem to respond better to naltrexone. Those with "positive family history of drinking", "subjective report of enhanced craving for alcohol" and "enhanced opioid activity" in response to alcohol ingestion for those with "specific genetic polymorphism at the mu opioid receptor".

The "average dose for naltrexone is 50 mg daily" and the most common side effect are the followings: "sedation, nausea, vomiting, dizziness and abdominal pain".

It is important to note that, "hepatocellular injury" has been associated, with high dose of naltrexone, in the range of 300 mg".

Therefore its use is contraindicated in patient wit acute liver disease or with liver enzymes greater than 3 times above normal as well as patients being treated with opiates, due to the risk of precipitating withdrawal.

"Disulfiram Aversive Conditioning": The rate of compliance to this approach is very low 20% or lower. We all know that medication adherence, is the key to the successful use of disulfiram in patients with alcoholism.

In order to be successful with this approach "these patients have to be highly motivated. Attend AA (Alcohol Anonymous), have a longer drinking history, are socially stable and cognitively motivated".

The possible side effects of disulfiram are: "headache, fatigue, allergic dermatitis, impotence, peripheral neuropathy, garlic-like after-taste and hepatitis".

It is "contraindicated in patients with abnormal liver functions, cardiovascular and cerebrovascular illnesses, and cognitive impairment". The elderly and the pregnant women are not probably ideal candidates for this compound.

At the normal range of 125 mg-500 mg/day, this is a medication that is considered safe and well tolerated.

It is important to remember that "Disulfiram" is also a medication that helps with Cocaine Addiction. In order to accomplish this function this product target a particular enzyme DBH, "Dopamine Beta Hydroxylase" that convert dopamine to norepinephrine and inhibits it, leading to an overflow of Dopamine producing an effect similar to a dopamine agonist like cocaine, therefore reducing the craving for cocaine which is itself a dopamine agonist.

In order to target alcohol addition, "Disulfiram" targets and inhibits a different enzyme "Aldehyde Dehydrogenase"(ADH), the enzyme that convert acetaldehyde to acetate, therefore producing an overflow of acetaldehyde which itself cause the "DER: "Disulfiram Ethanol Reaction" including: "headache, sweating, facial flushing, nausea, vomiting, tachycardia, hyperventilation, dyspnea and hypotension".

The "DER" (Disulfiram Ethanol Reaction) is an "aversive reaction" that serves to extinguish addictive behavior through punishment, negative reinforcement and negative counter-conditioning.

It could also cause a severe reaction including: "respiratory depression, cardiovascular collapse, arrhythmias, myocardial infarction, acute congestive heart failure, seizures, unconsciousness and death".

Finally even though I did not mention "Nicotine" in my initial list, I would probably commit a crime toward Humanity not to mention and elaborate on this so called "legal substance", the worst and the most deadly of all with the highest dead rate.

Nowadays there are so many strategies in place in order to fight this calamity.

Fist of all "Vaccine Therapy" represent a new "immunologic type of Pharmacotherapy" to treat addictive disorders such as "cocaine, methamphetamine and nicotine addiction".

The goal of "antibody therapy either by active or passive immunization" is to "prevent these substances of abuse from penetrating into the CNS via pharmacokinetic antagonism".

Some studies have demonstrated that "Nicotine Vaccination" "reduces nicotine distribution to the brain by 40-60% and decreases seeking in drugs reinstatement paradigms". Three nicotine vaccines are in development, and have been tested in humans in phase 1 and 2 trials.

So far, they have been reported to be safe and well tolerated.

The "Endogenous Cannabinoid System" has been implicated in the reinforcing properties of some drugs of abuse such as nicotine and Alcohol.

"Rimonabant" a "CB1 receptor antagonist" has been shown in preclinical studies to "diminish nicotine self-administration as well as to decrease the relapse to some conditioned cues".

In a US trial of approximately 800 smokers, "Rimanobant" has double the rate of abstinence. However the FDA did not approve it because of "concerns over report of depression, anxiety, insomnia and suicidal ideation".

"Combination therapy": It has been reported that adding "SNRI" to a longer-acting agent such as "Nicotine Patch", "Bupropion" or "Varenicline", could be used after mono-therapy have failed.

"Clonidine": an alpha2 adrenergic agonist that diminishes noradrenergic release and thus decreased sympathetic activation,

is thought to "counteract CNS manifestation of Nicotine withdrawals" as "Hyperadrenergic States" are common features across a spectrum of withdrawal syndromes including: "alcohol and opioids". This is a representation of the activation of the brain stress system. Some trials of clonidine used for smoking cessation demonstrate an approximate doubling of abstinence rate.

"Nortriptyline": A tricyclic antidepressant that acts as a NE reuptake inhibitor as well as a NAR antagonist. It could approximately double the rate of smoking cessation.

"Varenicline": most common side effects; "Nausea, insomnia, headache". Varenicline was associated with some serious adverse effects in the US including: "accidents and injuries, vision disturbances, arrhythmia, seizure, abnormal muscle spasms or movements, moderate and severe skin reactions like SJS (Stevens Johnson Syndrome), Diabetes and Neuro-Psychiatric symptoms like change of behaviors, agitation, suicidal ideation, attempted and completed suicide".

"Varenicline" is a long acting 24 hours partial agonist at the "alpha4beta2" NAR (Nicotinic Receptor). By being a partial agonist, it stimulates release of enough DA to reduce craving and withdrawal. In the presence of inhaled nicotine from tobacco it acts partially as an antagonist by blocking the full reinforcing effect of smoked tobacco.

In a phase 3 trial, verinicline 1mg bid was compared to bupropion SR 150 mg bid. After 12 weeks varenicline increased the odds of abstinence by a factor of two compared to bupropion.

Bupropion exerted its anti addictive properties in tobacco dependent patients as an "indirect result of its anti-depressant properties". It is considered as a first line agent used in the treatment of nicotine addiction.

There are 5 NRT (Nicotine Replacement Therapy) FDA approved for use in the US: I)"Transdermal patch", II)"Gum", III) "Lozenge", IV) "Nasal Spray" and V) "Vapor Inhaler".

I) The "Transdermal patch" is a long acting NRT (LANRT) that provides continuous release of Nicotine for 16-24 hours. II) The "Nasal Spray", III) "The Inhaler", IV) "The Gum" and V) "The Lozenge" on the other hand constitute the short-acting NRT (SANRT)

NRT's work via the "mechanism of agonist substitution", "reducing the reinforcing properties of nicotine delivery by tobacco", and also "reducing the severity of craving and withdrawal symptoms".

All the data previously listed, are excerpts of my scattered thoughts on the topic of addiction to the most common so-called legal drugs as well as the street drugs.

The inclusion of the "designer drugs" made the issue more difficult to tackle, since they are being generated so rapidly and are emerging almost everywhere in this country.

Thanks to the creativity of the drug dealers who are eager to maintain the "legal status" of their products since some newly crafted laws make them illegal as soon as they emerge on the market. Therefore they end up growing like mushrooms in an attempt to maintain their legal status. Because of their rapid evolution and emergence these designer drugs continue to outnumber the natural compounds.

H.C.B

01-17-15

The Hazards associated with Psychotropic Medications

There are a few potentially deadly disorders associated with the use of psychotropic medications.

We can mention some of them including: "Neuroleptic malignant Syndrome", "Serotonin Syndrome", "Torsade De Pointe", "Agranulocytosis", "Stevens Johnson Syndrome", "Parkinsonism", "Metabolic Syndrome" and "Tardive dyskinesia"

The "Neuroleptic malignant Syndrome" seems to be one of the most dangerous. It is characterized by the development of: "fever", "muscular rigidity", "autonomic instability", "altered level of consciousness", "elevated creatine kinase and creatine phosphokinase" (CK and CPK)" and "elevated white blood cell count" (WBC).

Moving to the "Serotonin Syndrome", it is a disorder often resulting from the simultaneous usage of different anti-depressive medications.

Using antidepressants such as the "Tricyclic Antidepressant" (TCA's), The "Selective Serotonin Reuptake Inhibitors" (SSRI's) or the "Mono Amine Oxidase Inhibitors" (MAOI's) concurrently can generate the syndrome.

This ailment is a very serious and potentially fatal condition, resulting from the different combinations described earlier; where some "TCA's" like "Imipramine and Desipramine" or some "MAOI's" like "Parnate or phenelzine" generate a severe form of the illness.

The syndrome itself is characterized by "tremors at rest", "hypertonicity" and "autonomic signs".

The patient suffering from this condition can also presents with "hallucinosis" and "hyperthermia" leading to death.

The next condition in line the "Torsade de Pointe" is a "deadly cardiac arrhythmia" which can occur with the use of certain types of neuroleptics such as: "Geodon (zyprazodone)", "Fanapt (Ileoperidone)", "Mellaril (thioridazine)" and "Seroquel (Quetiapine)".

These neuroleptics have the potential to increase the "QT-QTC interval of the electrocardiogram (EKG) beyond 500 ms (Milisecond)", inducing therefore this dangerous arrhythmia.

It is important to emphasize that this ailment is triggered by some other group of medications in addition to the "Neuroleptics". Indeed some other medications or combination of medications can also produce it.

Medications like "Ciprofloxacin" and "methadone" could induce this dangerous arrhythmia, because they too can increase the "Qt/Qtc interval" to a dangerously abnormal range.

Switching to an Hematologic Condition entitled: "Agranulocytosis" that could also turnout to be deadly, because it deprives the body from the ability to defend itself against infections by inhibiting the production of granulocytes which are part of the cellular immunity, causing therefor the body to become defenseless. This is a condition occurring mostly with the use of "clozaril", an atypical neuroleptic utilized to overcome "treatment resistant schizophrenia".

It is also important to emphasize that this disorder could naturally happen in certain ethnic group to create the so-called "Benign Ethnic Neutropenia" (BEN).

Continuing our exploration of the psychotropic medications that could be potentially harmful by inducing some deadly pathologic conditions; there is a dermatologic entity by the name of: "Stevens Johnson Syndrome" which usually comes with a partner named "Toxic Epidermal Necrolysis", that could even be more treacherous and devastating than the primary condition.

This is indeed a super dangerous skin condition occurring with: "general rashes", "fever" and "elevated WBC count". This disorder occurs with the use of the anti-seizure medication Lamotrigine (Lamictal) usually utilized to treat the "depressive phase of Bipolar Disorder", which is itself a phase of mood disorder where the sufferer is profoundly unhappy and could present with a high risk of suicide. It is also imperative to emphasize that most rashes caused by lamotrigine prove to be usually benign; as a rule "rashes" are the side effect that most often complicate treatment with this particular medication.

It is important for the clinician to be able to recognize the "hallmarks of serious life threatening rashes" which usually present with the following features: "confluent area of erythema", "facial edema", "skin pain", "blisters or epidermal detachment" the so-called "Positive Nikolsky's Sign" (easy separation of the outer layer of epidermis with the basal layer with thumb pressure), "mucus membrane erosion", "fever", "enlarged lymph nodes", "arthralgia or arthritis", "shortness of breath", "wheezing", "laryngeal edema", "elevated eosinophil count" and "abnormal LFT's (Liver Functions Tests)". Most benign rashes lack these features and are mostly "maculo-papular" in appearance. Some rashes that appear benign however may evolve in more serious one.

Therefore the rule of thumb for any patient on Lamotrigine who has any rash, is to report it immediately to the psychiatrist who must hold the next dose of the medication. It is critical to know that, this disorder usually happens when the medication is being titrated up to quickly.

The condition that follows is usually pretty common "Parkinsonism"; an ailment that has different subcomponents including: "pill-rolling tremors", "dystonic reaction", "rigidity" and "akathysia".

The "neuroleptic induced acute dystonia" is characterized by a "brief or prolonged spasm of certain muscle groups", depending of the muscle group involved, it generates such entities like: "Oculogyric Crisis" an involuntary contractions of the muscles of the eyes; "Tongue Protusion" involving the muscles of the tongue, "Torticolis" spasm involving the muscles of the neck, "Trismus" induced by the contraction of the muscle of the jaw and "Laryngo-Pharyngeal Dystonia" involving muscles of the pharynx and the larynx; finally the patient could present with some dystonic postures of the trunk and the limbs. These different subgroups of muscular spasms usually happen in young males under age 30 who are very bulky and muscular.

The "neuroleptic induced acute akathysia" is characterized, by a subjective or objective feeling of restlessness, a powerful urge to keep moving which could possibly be profoundly disabling and triggers some thought of suicide. The patient has often a "sense of anxiety", "an inability to relax"; some "jitteriness, pacing and rocking motion" while sitting and some rapid alternation of sitting and standing motion. Middle-aged women are often at risk for this condition.

Moving on the "Metabolic Syndrome", a condition induced by certain atypical neuroleptic like: "olanzapine" (zyprexa), "quetiapine" (Seroquel) and "clozapine" (clozaril). These medications affect the "Body Mass Index" (BMI) with subsequent increased of the different components of the lipid panel, mostly the "triglycerides" and the "low density lipoprotein" along with the "glycosylated hemoglobin" (Hba1c) with subsequent "diabetic Keto acidosis" (DKA).

The "Neuroleptic Induced Tardive Dyskinesia" or "Tardive Dyskinesia" (TD) for short, is a disabling movement disorder occurring, after the long-term use of certain neuroleptics mostly the traditional neuroleptic like: Haldol, Prolixin, Navane and Trilafon. This late appearing condition has a characterization of involuntary choreoathetoic movements targeting the "orofacial region", the fingers and the toes. Some movement of the head, the neck and the hips are also present. As a result, the patient ends up having some "breathing irregularities", some "dysphagia" or swallowing difficulties resulting in "aerophagia", belching and grunting.

This bleak clinical picture caused by the long term treatment with traditional neuroleptics target certain groups including: people with increased age (the elderly), female gender, and the presence of cognitive and mood disorders.

It is worth mentioning conditions like: "Hypertensive Episodes" manifested by the sudden occurrence of occipital headache subsequent to an "hypertensive crisis" in a patient taking an "MAOI", an absolute emergency.

This could also be caused by a "hypertensive hyperpyrexia reaction" seen mostly with people who took an overdose of "MAOI'S",

This peculiar picture can possibly be seen in combination with "Serotonin Syndrome" and "Hypertensive Crisis".

The "MAOI's" also interact adversely with several antihypertensive agents. A hypertensive crisis may result, from the use of an MAOI with a diet rich in "Tyramine".

As described previously the occurrence of combined: "hypertension", "hyper-arousal", "hyperthermia" and "severe myoclonus" possibly suggest "MAOI Overdose"

This is a list with the description of some hazardous conditions that could occur with the use of psychotropic medications.

We therefore need to stay vigilant, keep our radar active and raise the red flag as soon as we see an atypical reaction, while using any psychotropic medication in order to avoid a catastrophe.

H.C.B

01-09-15

The Pluses and Minuses of the New DSM

In my opinion, one of the major handicaps of the new DSM is the removal of what I deem is an important tool, a powerful weapon from the psychiatrist's availability. This tool in my view is his ability to summarize the patient history with the five axes.

The five axes, where usually the first three describe the psychiatric and the medical diagnosis, the fourth describes the stressors and the fifth the functionality and the degree of the patient's disability.

I also believe regardless of the rational expressed, the different subcategories of schizophrenias should be studied more deeply, instead of being discarded, since describing the different subcategories of the disorder is important. However, I agree with the discussion over the difficulty regarding the perception of what is bizarre vs. what is non bizarre which could be purely subjective.

Switching gear and moving on through the different changes observed in the DSM-V, I think the substitution of (NOS) "not otherwise specified" by the word "specified" and/or "unspecified" is quite appropriate.

In addition the replacement of Autistic Disorders

(Asperger Disorder, Childhood Disintegrative Disorder, and Pervasive Development Disorder) by ASD (Autism Spectrum disorder) is justified because of the confusion created sometime for the clinicians when an attempt at differentiating the different subcategories of the syndrome is made.

Going through the multiple changes implemented in DSM-V, replacing "Mental Retardation" by "Intellectual Disability Disorder" put a greater emphasis on the adaptive functional deficit, rather than the IQ scores. In addition the connotation behind the word "Mental Retardation" and its demeaning implication has been rightfully eliminated.

The age of onset of ADHD (Attention Deficit Hyperactivity Disorder) was raised from 7 to 12, because people have a tendency to give in to school pressure, wanting to diagnose the condition at age 7 while some studies had proven otherwise.

According to these studies, the disorder starts later in the patient's life and is not seen as diffusely in early childhood.

In addition the symptoms threshold for adults age 17 and older was reduced to five instead of the large number described before. There is a logical explanation for this, since patients have fewer symptoms in adulthood than in childhood.

Considering the learning disability subgroup "Specific Learning Disorder" summarize all the different types of learning disorder since most children with this conditions have deficit in more than one area including: reading, writing and mathematics.

Going to the SchizoAffective Disorders, they are now based on the lifetime duration of the illness, rather than an episodic duration. In the DSM-IV the language regarding the duration of the illness was quite ambiguous and confusing for the mental health professional.

It is worth mentioning among he major changes that "Catatonia" now exist as a specifier for neurodevelopmental, psychotic, mood and other mental or medical disorders.

Lastly the use of the term "neurocognitive disorders" rather than Dementia seems more descriptive, since the term dementia is usually associated with neurocognitive disorders exclusively in older populations e.g. "Alzheimer's Dementia" and "Lewis Body Dementia".

However some neurocognitive disorders, occur in Young Adult e.g. "TBI (Traumatic Brain Injury)" and "AIDS-Dementia Complex".

Based on this streamlined review, it is clearly documented that there are some positives as well as some negatives underlined in the new DSM in my opinion, but the positives seem to have outweigh the negatives.

H.C.B

01-09-15

Pseudo Bulbar Affect and Traumatic Brain Injury

"Pseudo Bulbar Affect" is characterized by some "sudden involuntary outbursts of crying alternated with laughing". This neurological condition often force the sufferers to be homebound, because they usually do not want to leave their houses by fear of having a sudden, unexpected crying and laughing spells that could be embarrassing to them.

They are just like some patients suffering from "Panic Disorder" with agoraphobia who usually are homebound by fear of having a panic attack, when they happen to be in an open crowded space where they believe escaping or egressing would be impossible to them.

These bouts of crying and laughing spell could occur several times a day and last from several seconds to several minutes. And just like panic attacks these crying and laughing episodes usually have no trigger and happen out of the blue.

This condition is also known as "Emotional Incontinence" and "Pathological crying and laughing" which seem to be quite an accurate description.

"Pseudo Bulbar affect" is not just a manifestation of TBI (Traumatic Brain injury) even though it is often reported in this condition.

It could also happen in many other neurological conditions, including: "ALS" (Amyotrophic Lateral Sclerosis), "MS" (Multiple Sclerosis), "Parkinson Disease" and some variety of "Strokes".

In addition to their being homebound, the subjects with "Pseudo Bulbar Affect" have poor social interaction and become lonely, because they avoid interacting with family and friends and are hardly able to function. Some of them get divorced or break intimate relationships in which they were involved. Because of the gradual degradation of their living situation they end up in a supervised living scenario. They become frustrated and one the most striking feature of their presentation is that their "crying and laughing" is incongruent with their usual mood state. The quality of the crying in patients with "PBA", usually come across as "a weeping with or without tears", a sobbing or a wailing or even a crying with inarticulate sound. This peculiar type of crying can happen in Dementia and be mischaracterized as behavioral disturbances in the demented individual.

It may also be mistaken for depression, which can coexist with "PBA". "Post stroke depression" with "post stroke behavioral changes" is another condition where one can find this pattern of crying being imitated. It could be found in PTSD as well.

"Nuedextra (Detrometorphan Hbr + Quinidine sulfate)" is a combined medication that seems to work in "PBA" regardless of the neurological condition associated with it including: "ALS", "MS", "TBI", "PD"

The "quinine sulfate" component is being used at 1-3% of the dose recommended for cardiac arrhythmia. It is a metabolic inhibitor allowing therapeutic dose of "dextromethorphan", by increasing its plasma concentration and prolonging its half-life by 2 to 13 hours.

It is important to emphasize that it can also cause some dose dependent "QTC Prolongation" with the risk of causing a "Torsade de Pointe" which is a deadly cardiac arrhythmia. Therefore an EKG must be performed 3-4 hours after the first dose.

"Nuedexta 20mg/10mg" can modulate glutamate in two major ways 1) by presynaptic inhibition of glutamate release; and 2) by postsynaptic glutamate response modulation.

This medication according to some study benefit about 75% of patient with "Pseudo Bulbar Affect"

We clearly can see that there is a great deal of hope for patients suffering from such a disabling condition. This hope could be even greater if this biological intervention can be combined, with some psychosocial approaches.

H.C.B
06-04-15

"Varenicline", another option for the treatment of Alcohol dependence

"Varenicline "(Chantix), "a partial alpha4 beta2 nicotinic acetylcholine agonist" (NAA) officially indicated for Nicotine Addiction has reduced drinking in some animal and small human studies.

The "Nicotine Acetylcholine Receptor" (NAR) plays a significant role in the "rewarding effect of both nicotine and alcohol" which makes it a target in the treatment of both disorders; therefore creating another option for the treatment of Alcohol dependence in addition to those already established such as: "Disulfiram" (Antabuse), "Naltrexone" (Revia and Vivitrol), "Acamprosate" (Campral) and more recently "Gabapentin" (Neurontin).

The attractive segment of this treatment approach is that, it allows one to targets with one single chemical projectile, two deadly and chronic entities. It is like killing two birds with one stone, the two birds being the Alcohol Addiction and the Nicotine Addiction the single stone being "Varenicine".

We frequently come across individuals stricken, afflicted by both conditions; for them it could be very convenient to be able to treat these disabling, lethal and chronic illnesses by a single weapon.

The authors of this study published by NIH (National Institute of Health) suggest that, before making it a formal approach for the management of Alcohol Dependence, more researches need to be done in order to replicate the trial result.

There some serious heath benefits associated to the concomitant reduction of drinking and smoking. There is indeed a major decrease of medical diseases, aggression and alcohol related deaths.

In spite of the black box warning ascribed to this compound (Varenicline), in this study the product did not increase suicidal ideation, mood change, thoughts or behavior changes (hostility or agitation). However some GI (Gastro intestinal) side effects such as nausea constipation were registered.

This could overall be contemplated as a positive profile, when one will have to consider the risks vs. the tremendous benefits connected to this compound if and when one has to take it into consideration.

H.C.B

06-11-15

The use of Gabapentin for Alcohol Dependence

There are many established treatments for Alcohol Dependence including the use of the aversive compound: "Disulfiram" (Antabuse), which many people involved in the treatment of this condition, find very dangerous because of its side effect profile. There are hopefully some other modalities of treatment that seem to make wonders in the management of Alcohol Dependence.

Some people use "Naltrexone" an opioid blocker approved by the FDA (Federal Drug Administration) for this purpose even though, it can also be use in the treatment of "Opioid Dependence". This is an approach that can indeed be used for this disorder, in addition to Methadone and Buprenorphine. There is an oral form for this compound (Revia) and a long term injectable or depot form (Vivitrol), administered every 4 weeks once we realize that allergy is not an issue with this chemical. This approach can be utilized up to six months. Once we transition to the depot, we needs to make sure our patients wear a bracelet with the purpose of alerting any health care professionals involved in any case of emergency, where the patient could possibly face a surgical intervention or any other invasive procedure. This is in order to let them know that, the patient is on a "long term opioid blocker" potentially capable to antagonize any opioid agonist given to him as an anesthetic agent, whether oral or systemic designed to relieve pain.

Being cognizant of this fact, the practitioner should be able to use an alternative strategy for pain-relieved purposes. It is also important to emphasize that the patient must have a healthy liver in order to be able to receive this product because of its negative hepatic impact such as increased of the liver enzymes. Therefore liver functions tests must be performed periodically for patients taking this medication.

Another medication that is also officially indicated for "Alcohol Dependence" "Acamprosate" Campral, is exclusively metabolized by the kidney and could be an alternative treatment for this chronic and tedious condition in case of liver disease, a clear contraindication for "Naltrexone" and "Disulfiram" for that matter.

This medication has the potential of using a different metabolic pathway via the kidney targeting the glutamate receptors, completely avoiding the liver.

Focusing on "Gabapentin" as an agent that helps in the treatment of "Alcohol Dependence", it has been reported that "early abstinence" is associated with the activation of the "Brain Stress System" in the Amygdala. "Protracted Abstinence" therefore may involve symptoms of craving, mood and sleep disturbances, which are all risks for relapse.

"Gabapentin" a medication officially approved by the FDA for the treatment of epileptic seizure and neuropathic pain, "blocks a specific alpha-2 subunit of the voltage gated calcium channel at selective presynaptic site", and as a result modulates "Gamma Amino Butyric Acid" (Gaba) neurotransmission. According to some recently done studies Gabapentin normalizes the "Stress induced activation in the Amygdala" associated with Alcohol Dependence. Therefore this is an excellent rational for its evaluation in the treatment of this disorder. It turns out as per this study, that Gabapentin indeed reduces Alcohol cues craving and sleep disturbances in Alcohol dependent participants. It reduces not only craving, but also disturbances of sleep and mood in up to 42 to 44.7 % of patients when utilized at the dose range of 900 mg -1800 mg per day.

This study clearly shows that our arsenal therapeutic against "Alcohol Dependence" is slowly growing over time by the addition of new weapons such as the use of gabapentin and varenicline.

H.C.B

06-09-15

Cannabis and abnormalities of the "Nucleus Accumbens" and "Amygdala" in the Youth

According to some recently done researches, the "left nucleus accumbens" and the "right amygdala" are increased in size in the young patient using Cannabis. The "Anterior Cingulate Gyrus" usually implicated in craving, was not involved in this study. It is also reported that the "Hippocampus" considered as the major center for memory and possibly learning, could also be affected by the drug in young, immature under developed brains.

A secondary metabolite for THC, "THC-COOH" can be detected in the user's urine many weeks after the last use of the drug. It is therefore not considered a good marker for "Acute Marijuana Intoxication" usually associated with "increased resting heart rate" usually perceived by the user as "feeling his heart is jumping out of his chest".

In addition some other commonly observed signs are: "congestion of the conjunctiva blood vessels", "slow speech response" and "giddiness". It is reported that the number of joints smoked per occasion seems to be the only attribute greatly associated with changes in the "Nucleus Accumbens volume". Therefore the more joints are used the more extensive the damage done to the "Nucleus Accubens" will be.

Marijuana used may be associated with a disruption of the neural organization in some part of the "Nucleus Accumbens".

Some "subcortical structures" may be affected as well including: the "Thalamus".

There is an increased in the number of "dendritic branches" and "dendritic spines" in the shell of the "Nucleus Accumbens" in THC exposed rats. Some other studies have shown a volume reduction in the "Hippocampus", the "Amygdala" and the "Cerebellum".

The "Striatum", the "Orbital frontal Cortex", the "Parietal and the Occipital Cortex" are all areas affected by this chemical that is being legalized in many states in this country and is being considered innocuous, harmless.

Another Finding is the fact that the "surface of the Amygdala" was deformed inward with some "changes in the density of the prefrontal cortex bilaterally". The density of the gray matter in many areas of the brain is greater in marijuana users, in certain area such as the "left nucleus accumbens". This anomaly is being extended to the "subcallosal cortex", the "hypothalamus", the "sublenticular extended amygda" and the "left amygdala".

Marijuana is traditionally the most commonly used illicit drug in the united Stated. The multi-state legalization of this compound in the US will make its use more frequent than it has ever been before; extending therefore the damages caused by this drugs. These damages that are most prominent in the youth, with propensity for "psychotic conditions" including schizophrenia, for "anxiety attacks" including: "panic disorder", and for "mood disorders" including the so-called 'Amotivational Syndrome". The most significant damages are perhaps the perpetual injuries caused on the immature brain, that translate mostly in extremely diminished cognitive and intellectual abilities, reminding one of patients suffering from "Intellectual disabilities".

There are some medical claims, where marijuana has some therapeutic properties for people with glaucoma, by decreasing the intra-ocular pressure in the eyes. It also has some benefits in patients who undertake chemotherapy, by controlling the nausea and vomiting induced by the noxious medications used to treat some malignancies. Marijuana in addition has the ability to increase the appetite and improve the weight of cachectic patients suffering from HIV or some variety of cancers like pancreatic cancer.

All of these benefits would have had some values if they were used exclusively for these conditions without any diversions; otherwise the negatives heavily outweigh the positives resulting from the use of this compound.

H.C.B
06-13-15

Prescribed medications and false positivity during drugs testing

There are reportedly a large number of prescribed medications that could induce false positivity in drugs testing.

Some of these data are scientifically proven, but others unfortunately are not.

According to some statistics the occurrence of these false- positive results are in the range of 5%-10% even though some people would wish these figures were higher.

However on the flip side, some new researches show some falsely negative results as well allowing some individuals to get away with their use of street drugs.

Some categories of medications including: antihistamines, antidepressants, antibiotics, analgesics, antipsychotics and some over the counter agents, can all be implicated.

Amphetamine or methamphetamine was the most commonly reported false positive UDS (Urine Drugs Screen) results, mostly because of similarity in the chemical structure of amphetamine and ephedrine. However these false positive tests also happen paradoxically in agents that are not structurally related.

"Ranitidine" by example, which is structurally dissimilar to amphetamine, can give false positive result for amphetamine and methamphetamine; "Brompheniramine" a medication used for seasonal allergy and vasomotor rhinitis can also produce false positive result for amphetamine.

"Dextromethorphan" an opioid derivative used to control cough, instead of giving false positive result for opioid, gives false positive result for "Phencyclidine or PCP".

There are some reports of false positivity for PCP with "Ibuprofen".

"Naproxen" could give false positive result for "Cannabinoids" and "Barbiturates". This reportedly could also happen with "Ibuprofen".

False positive result for methadone and opiates can occur with "Diphenhydramine" and "Doxylamine" a non-prescription nasal inhaler, "l-desoxyephedrine" can give false positivity for "Amphetamine".

The use of "Quinolone Derivatives" particularly "Levofloxacin" and "Ofloxacin" could possibly induce false positivity for opioid. "Rifampin" is another antibiotic that could be associated with false positive result for opioids.

The "Phenothiazine" particularly "Promethazine" can give false positive result for "Amphetamine". "Chlorpromazine" can produce the same result, inducing false positivity for amphetamine. "Quetiapine" an atypical neuroleptic was associated with false positive result for methadone

"Bupropion" an aminoketone structurally related to phenylethylamine can possibility give false positive results for "Amphetamine".

"Sertraline" an SSRI (Selective Serotonin Reuptake Inhibitor) could give false positive result for benzodiazepine.

"Selegeline" an MAOI could provide false positive result for "Amphetamine and Methamphetamine", so is "Trazodone" a triazolopyridine.

"Venlafaxine" an SNRI (Serotonin Norepinephrine Reuptake Inhibitor) can be falsely positive for "PCP".

Finally "Verapamil" a "calcium channel blocker" possibly can produce falsely positive result for "Methadone".

In addition it is well known that eating a teaspoon of "Poppy Seeds" can trigger false positive result on tests for opioid abuse.

I believe that knowing the limitations in the testing methods for some drugs of abuse is critical, since some important forensics decisions are being made based on the results of these tests. These decisions are made in the legal system and people can be sent to jailed or have longer probation period depending on these results.

These decisions are also made in the sport arena and some athlete's career can be ruined because of them.

On a larger scale some people can be fired and therefore lose their job, their only mode of survival depending on the results of these tests.

That is one the reason why physicians by and large must be aware of these findings. We need to remember that cold medications like "Dextromethorphan" can falsely test positive for "Phencyclidine" (PCP) as mentioned previously.

Antidepressants like "Wellbutrin" or even some "Tricyclic Antidepressants" can falsely test positive for "Amphetamines".

"Zoloft" and "Daypro" (Oxaprozin) a medication used for osteoarthritis and rheumatoid arthritis can give some problems by being falsely positive for "Benzodiazepine"

"Quinolones Antibiotics" like "Cipro" which is frequently used in urinary tract infections, can induce false positive results for Opioids" according to some studies.

Some "HIV Medications" can show up in these tests as if the subject were using "Marijuana".

Strangely there are not many false positive results reported with "Cocaine". However false positive results for "Amphetamines and Methamphetamine" were the most commonly reported.

False positive results for methadone, opioids, phencyclidine barbiturates, cannabinoids, and benzodiazepines were also reported as mentioned in the numerous cases listed previously.

It is also imperative to know that the most common tests used to screen urine for drugs of abuse are "immunoassays" and a large number of false positive results have been reported by the use of these methods; which is why these tests must be confirmed by using additional analytic methods such as: "gas chromatography" and "mass spectrometry".

The verification of the results originating from these rapid screening products should be the rule of thumb, since the use of medications with the potential for false-positive "UDS (Urine Drugs Screen)" possibly present a liability for individuals who are required to do random UDS as a component of a recovery in certain programs like a court ordered monitoring program or as a condition for employment.

H.C.B

06-18-15

Transcranial Near-Infrared Therapy, a new neuro-modulation technic for Depression

This new "electrical" or "neuro-modulation" modality is still in progress and is not considered prime time yet.

However the preliminary results are encouraging after being tested by some instruments like "The Hamilton Depression rating scale" and "The Hamilton anxiety scale score".

An article in the journal of "Clinical Psychiatry News" written by Debra L Beck describes this non-invasive therapy, which works by enhancing the brain's bio-energetic metabolism and offer a treatment alternative to patients with refractory symptoms of Depression.

Transcranial Near-Infrared (NIR) light passes through the skull and stimulates "Cytochrome C Oxidase" within the mitochondria, which as a result increases energy production and has some anti-inflammatory property. According to Dr. Nieremberg a psychiatrist at Massachusetts General Hospital and Harvard Medical School, "Transcranial Near-Infrared Light"

is extremely neuro-protective and has shown real promise in the treatment of "Traumatic Brain Injury "(TBI) and is being studied to treat Mood Disorder.

Some pilot studies are full of promises in people with Major Depression and Anxiety after about 2 weeks of therapy.

As mentioned before some screening tools such as the "Hamilton Depression Scale" and the "Hamilton Anxiety Scales Score" were able to measure objectively the positive impact of this therapeutic approach. A fair amount of regression was observed at four weeks pass treatment. However it is not known yet however whether people could repeat exposure after an initial attempt.

In addition there is a "Transcranial Laser Therapy" that is being studied as well for the treatment of Major Depressive Disorder. Dr. Nieremberg made some additional remarks when he states that; "Near-Infrared Therapy" is not about sun light exposure, since there is not enough infrared spectrums in regular sunlight. This new therapeutic approach, perceived in the horizon is slowly shaping itself into a solid therapeutic modality. This will enlarge the list of "neuro- modulation technics" that will be ready to take over in case of failure of our traditional chemical or pharmacological arsenals.

H.C.B

07-01-15

The Biological aspect of Depression And Suicide

Some new studies have emphasized the biological aspect of Depression and Suicide according to an article written by Carmen Blake and Brian J Miller in the journal of Biological Psychiatry. When these studies will be completed and become prime time perhaps a new era will start for Biological Psychiatry.

Some psychiatric illnesses will be diagnosed just like medical sicknesses when these new data will be solidly implemented.

According to these studies, a great deal of psychiatric syndromes is associated with "inflammation and aberrant cytokine and chemokine levels", including Depression with suicidal ideation when compared to control.

There was indeed some evidence of "aberrant cytokine levels in the blood and the cerebrospinal fluid" of these patients who for the most part suffer from Depression with fleeting suicidal ideation as we mentioned previously.

In addition "post mortem brain samples" of patients who died by suicide, reflect these findings. Furthermore the levels of "Interleukin-1Beta" (IL-1B) and "Interleukin-6" (IL-6) were robustly associated with Suicidality and were increased in the blood of these patients.

In vitro level of "Interleukin-2" (IL-2) production by peripheral blood mononuclear cells however was significantly decreased in patients with suicidality, when compared to those without suicidality and healthy controls.

The levels of "interleukin-8" (IL-8) in the "cerebrospinal fluid" of suicidal versus control subjects were also significantly decreased. Rigorously designed longitudinal studies are intensely needed to evaluate these links further.

The wonders and the positive scientific aspects of these studies, are the hope that these "cytokines" may help in the near future distinguish suicidal from non-suicidal patients. Therefore a single lab test, combined with the usual habitual clinical symptoms that are part of our diagnostic procedure, will confirm whether somebody suffering from Depression is really suicidal.

Consequently it will become very appealing to realize we can diagnose Depression with Suicide the same way we confirm a condition like myocardial infarction by ordering some cardiac enzymes or the level of troponin in the blood. For our depressed and suicidal patients, we could order a blood level of Interleukin- 1B "IL-1B" and Interleukin-6 "IL-6" with the purpose of confirming our diagnosis.

This could be one of the major steps in the Development of Biological Psychiatry, transforming a subjective, evasive branch of Medicine to a solid objective, biological part of the Medical Science, creating therefore another revolution in the field of Psychiatry.

H.C.B

07-14-15

Chapter 11:
Human Interaction

_Terror for Young Black Males in America

_The strengths and weaknesses
of Human Interaction

Terror for young Black Males in America

This above title or statement is not an empty one, since there is apparently some "psychology of terror" in young black males living in America following the shooting, beating and killing of so many of them, by the Police over the past couple of years. This very sad reality seems to have a psychological impact even on the youngest among them. There are even some stories regarding very young black males in the range of 6 years old, who state that they do not want to be black anymore since they are convince they will be killed by the Police. In some cases when young black males come across some officers patrolling the streets, they avoid making eye contact, and some of them have a tendency to run for their safety while they have done nothing wrong. By so doing, they attract the attention and the wrath of some officers, who erroneously believe they must be guilty of something, anything; and they decided to go after them triggering their death accidentally sometime, but occasionally they are deliberately killed, intentionally murdered. The fact that these incidents involve White officers in most cases, reminds one of a somber chapter in the history of this country when "Black People" were being killed in large numbers by Whites and treated like animals rather than "Human Beings". This tendency is probably the phenomenology of a deeper, more extensive social problem, reflecting the secular division between blacks and whites in America. We all know this schism has some multiple and profound roots that appear to have been in resurgence lately while having a devastating impact on our youngsters by poisoning their mind. The end result is to terrorize the very young who having no maturity and no insight into what is going on, wish that the color of their skin were different.

H.C.B

05-10-15

The Strengths and Weaknesses of Human Interaction

Human Interaction can be beneficial in many ways.

When we as Human beings know that we can depend on someone, this can be very soothing for most of us.

In the field of Psychiatry, when a patient knows he/she has a support system, this can have a powerful therapeutic impact and facilitates his recovery.

In some cases even the company of a pet can do wonders for a lonely hopeless individual.

As a result the subject becomes able to cope better and has a chance to come as close as possible to his previous level of functioning.

He does have a chance to feel less withdrawn and become more expansive, more outgoing, and livelier. He feels like he does have a second chance at living and surviving. He feels like he is being born again, born de novo. All these remarks listed, can be considered as some of the strengths of Human Interaction.

However it is not always positive since it can also be disastrous, deadly, and vicious. We know this very well since we have seen some cases with this outcome and we then speak about HEE (High expressed Emotion) for the patient.

Nothing can be more devastating for a psychiatric patient than when a member of his support system becomes highly critical, insensitive and callous toward him. This outcome could decrease or eliminate all chances at regaining even a fraction of his previous level of functioning. This could push him to fall in a ditch, a trench, a hole where he ends up experiencing the deepest feeling of anhedonia and hopelessness that could lead him to suicide, which is the worse scenario for him.

Based on this assertion, Human Interaction could go either way. That is why it is very important to do some psycho education for the patient's family or anybody who is part of his support system. It is very important to let everybody know that he is sick, profoundly sick sometime. He is just sick, not lazy not filthy not dirty; neither does he have a taste for bad sanitation, bad hygiene. He is just bizarre because of his illness and what he really needs is some encouragement to get over this rocky path. This stony and pebbly road that he must follow and overcome in order to have a chance at surviving and coping with the demands of every day life.

Human Interaction as we know it could objectively has some strength, but it can also have some disastrous and devastating weaknesses.

H.C.B

09-07-15

Chapter 12: Emotional, Sexual and Abusive Relationships

_The perpetuity of Emotional, Sexual and Physical Abuse in Human Beings

The Perpetuity of Emotional, Sexual and physical Abuse in Human Beings

Abuses as a rule regardless of their nature, whether they are sexual, emotional, or physical, can break the spirit of the recipient and leave him/her with some scars that remain indelible. It is important to realize, contrarily to the belief of some people; abuses are not just physical or sexual, they could be just emotional or they could include all of the above. It is important to know that emotional abuses can be as treacherous as deadly as the other kinds of abuses. In some cases they could be even worse, since they can break the spirit of the abuse and take away, remove all his/her desire to enjoy live, leaving behind some hideous, unsightly scars. These scars although invisible, remain alive even when the sufferer attempts to have some sleep, since the picture, the ghosts symbolizing the abuse come back to life and keep refueling themselves. They become alive and keep reenacting themselves, becoming nightmares that are as vivid as the initial events. As a result the emotional impacts remain permanent, undying, everlasting. The people affected have most of the time lose all abilities to trust or they become gullible, incredibly naïve and vulnerable. In spite of the fact their ability to trust has been annihilated, defeated, and overpowered, in some cases the lost of this ability paradoxically make some of them lose their intellect as well and they open themselves to have more abuses inflicted on their body with a total disregard for their safety.

In some other circumstances the permanent excruciating emotional pain can occasionally and miraculously be relieve by their faith, allowing therefore some higher power to succeed when we all have failed as Human Beings. This higher spirit can therefore heal what we all have been powerless at healing.

This numbing that follows some time is like a sudden death of their soul following the trauma, and they become unable to have any animation from their broken spirit. And their immediate family is the first to be affected by their witnessing the spiritual death of their loved one. There is a certain isolation that follows, since the abuse becomes easily startled by anything reminding him of the original trauma and he/she becomes so frightened that he develops some avoidant behavior withdrawing in his shell the only place where he feels secured. Whenever he possibly can, he throws a retrospective look at his childhood or his early adulthood and perceives either of these of these periods, as a time when they were assaulted, annihilated by the abuser who is often a disgusting, appalling and unscrupulous individual.

Overtime no matter the intensity of the psychotherapeutic intervention utilized, these patients will never be the same; since they have been deprived of something nobody can give back to them "their childhood" or the "early part of their adult life" when they are still considered innocent and pure.

All of these mentioned earlier, all that were enumerated are gone, disappeared forever. When later in life the abuse could possibly "identify with the abuser" by some sort of psychological dynamic, they themselves could become abusers. However when on the contrary, they identify with their role as a victim, they seem to enjoy the "victim character" by some sort of masochism phenomenon, and end up having no will power, no stamina to defend themselves opening their body and spirit to absorb more atrocities, more cruelties, more mistreatments more abuses.

H.C.B

09-07-15

Chapter 13: Psychotherapy and Psychotherapy Subtypes

_Motivational Therapy

_Inter-Personal Therapy

_Dialectic Behavioral Therapy: (DBT)

Motivational Therapy

Motivational Therapy (MT) or Motivational Enhanced Therapy (MET), is a psychotherapeutic approach designed for people with Alcohol and Drugs addiction. These are conditions that are incredibly difficult to treat, and it is therefore important for the therapist not to come across as pressuring an already ambivalent and reluctant patient into treatment.

Individuals who are addicted to drugs and alcohol are usually, generally hesitant, undecided about getting rid of their habit. They often ask themselves whether they should do it or not, and they often procrastinate in their decision making process. That is the reason why Addiction generally is very challenging to treat and often ends up being a chronic illness.

Motivational Enhancement therapy (MET) is a patient centered counseling method that attempt to initiate "behavior change" by helping patients resolve their ambivalence about engaging in treatment and stopping their addition to drugs and alcohol. This tactic employs strategies to evoke rapid and internally motivated changes in the subject, rather than guiding him stepwise through the recovery process. This particular therapy provides feedback generated from an initial assessment to stimulate discussion regarding personal substance use and by doing so elicit self-motivational statements. Motivational interviewing principles are used to strengthen motivation for change. The changes, which will bring him away from the routine the vicious cycle in which he is trapped because of his addiction. The changes he is so afraid of implementing, because he will be deprived from the hedonic state of his addiction he enjoys so much.

Coping strategies for high risks situations are suggested and discussed with the addict. Over time the therapist monitors the changes, reviews the cessation strategies that are being used and continues to encourage a certain commitment to change and /or to sustain abstinence. The subject is encouraged to bring a "significant other" to the sessions occasionally for support, a strategy that can be powerful.

It could also backfire, if the "significant other" is not educated about the process and ends up putting pressure on the patient.

When things go smoothly, this approach could be a success.

According to certain statistics, this method has been successful in subjects addicted to alcohol and cannabis.

Having to decide freely without any pressure or any prompt, is probably one of the reasons why this modality of therapy has been so effective with some individuals dependent on alcohol and street drugs.

H.C.B
08-26-15

Interpersonal Therapy
Another type of therapy

There are a large variety of psychotherapeutic interventions,

"Interpersonal Therapy" is the subtype that is officially targeting some depressive disorders.

One of the corner stones of this condition so widely disseminated seems to be a flaw in interpersonal behavior.

It seems to derive from a flaw in the patient ability to interact with others; in other word there is a shortcoming in his interpersonal behavior.

Myrna, Weissman and Gerald, Klerman concocted this therapeutic approach after they realized that, improving interpersonal behavior can indeed improve these depressive disorders, since the patient will probably not feel as lonely and isolated as before.

This could be a powerful tool to have, in the treatment of depression, a condition that could be occasionally crippling and deadly.

We all know about the power and the benefit of human interaction, which in a way is an interpersonal exchange between human beings.

The depressed patient very often feels lonely, isolated, abandoned and has a tendency to maintain their "status"

That the reason why in this type of therapy the patients are taught objectively about their interaction with others and become aware of their tendency to isolate themselves which is a major contributor in making their depression worse. There is absolutely no focus on the transference and the therapist must attempt to be supportive, empathic and flexible. Some studies on the science behind this method have shown, in some cases of depressive disorders, (ITP) "Interpersonal Therapy" is favorably compared to "Biological Therapy" including the use of anti depressant medications.

Depressive Disorders could be crippling and deadly as mentioned previously and "ITP" could be a blessing and a life saver for the depressed, withdrawn and isolated patient.

H.C.B

04-06-15

Dialectic Behavioral Therapy (DBT)

The so-called "Diabetic behavioral therapy" or (DBT) for short is a therapeutic technic that was designed and developed by Marsha Lineham for patients suffering from (BPD) "Borderline Personality disorder". Being a subtype of "cognitive behavioral therapy", like all cognitive behavioral therapy approaches, the therapists involved in this subtype of therapy must be very active.

We know that the patient suffering from BPD, has a constellation, an agglomeration of symptoms which could be summarized as: 1) affective instability (Emotional), 2) self-injurious behavior (Behavioral), 3) evaluation and devaluation of others (Interpersonal).

We also know, even though it may not always be the case, this condition derives from a maladaptive pattern of attachment to parental figures resulting from abuse, neglect, emotional under-involvement and invalidation by caretakers.

One of the hallmarks of this disorder is that they are often in crisis with risk of suicide and self-injurious behavior, which is a "cry for help", a way for them to prevent abandonment and keep their "partner", their "other half", or whomever they are attached to, intimately linked to them. In other word this could be considered as a "resounding cry for help" as mentioned previously.

According to some statistics, 10% of patients with BPD commit suicide after they deem life is not worth living, after they realize the ghosts of their childhood continue to hunt them, after they realized they have not been validated and they have no hope for validation.

When they are in an "inpatient unit" they are incline to violence because they often can cope with other patients in the unit and also because of their tendency to idealize and devaluate people around them.

(DBT) "Dialectic Behavioral Therapy" is a therapeutic approach that really seems to work for this group of patients who are generally difficult to treat and are at time unpredictable and impulsive.

This psychotherapeutic method characterizes itself by:

1) Weekly skill training

2) Weekly individual therapy

3) Telephone skills consultations

4) Weekly consultations team by DBT therapists.

Patients in DBT, a psychotherapeutic approach that usually lasts about a year, are trained to "think and behave flexibly in accordance of what is needed".

DBT is a "Cognitive Behavioral Therapy" emphasizing the "acquisition and generalization" of a wide range of "cognitive and behavioral skills". One of the goals of DBT is to help the patient build a healthy life worth living.

Therefore DBT helps the patient develop a wide range of "essential life skills" in order to:

Decrease or even eliminate "behavioral dyscontrol". The focus therefore is in the "cognition or belief system" in order to target the "emotion and the behavior". One of the basic rule (CBT) "Cognitive Behavioral Therapy" is that your "cognition or belief system" will reflected in your "feelings of emotion" which will direct your "behavior". "Positive belief" will trigger "euphoric, positive feelings" that will be reflected in "appropriate, constructive, non disruptive behavior".

It increases value driven life style and promotes behavioral changes.

The patient uses many different tools including:

A "Primary Treatment Manuel" and: some "Group Skills". In DBT, "dialectical thinking" influences the "therapist world" and the process by which "therapeutic changes" occur.

All cognitive behavioral therapy approaches focus indeed as mentioned previously, on the "thinking process" in order to change the "feeling" and the "behavior".

The "dialectical thinking" is a form of "rational thinking" designed to bring "changes" in the behavior.

In order to use this strategy, the therapist must understand himself, the patient, and the world by applying the principles of Cognitive Behavior Therapy.

The "patient's behavior" is conceptualized in order to understand him/her. The "dialectical process of change" which is a direct consequence of "dialectical thinking" helps "changes the patient" and by the same mechanism, the "therapist behavior and cognition".

In order to use the "dialectical process" in DBT, the therapists work with the patient to create "a synthesis".

The "Dialectical Process" allows both the patient and the therapist to explore together what plan makes the most sense, or is the most effective in any given context. Since neither the patient nor the therapist, is right or wrong.

"Skills plan and practices" overtime allow the patient to broaden his "behavioral repertoire" in order to become "more flexible and effective" in the real world. Therefore for the patient with "BPD", this "repeated dialectical change" is thought to help reduce "rigid and extreme maladaptive patterns of behavior and thinking". The "fundamental of dialectic" in DBT is: "Acceptance" and "Change".

For the "BPD patient", the core principles of "acceptance and change", requires that he/she learn to accept "painful emotions and thoughts" as they exist in the moment, recognize they are occurring, and understand their functions.

The patient must understand that "anger makes him/her yell at this person". Once he acknowledges this, he/she works to change "dysfunctional responses" to these experiences.

The changing context of each moment inspires "Acceptance" and the "Possibility for Subsequent Changes".

Therefore DBT could be summarized throughout its practice as the: "Acceptance and Change Dialectic". In other word acknowledging how realizing that the "thought of anger", triggers the "feeling of being angry" and the "dysfunctional behavior" of: yelling, screaming, threatening and when at the extreme: assaulting".

It is however not an easy process, this "dialectical balancing act" could become a "catch 22" covering different goals; as in all 'cognitive behavior therapy" it comes with "rehearsal" in order to make it possible.

From one hand it helps the patient use "Acceptance base skills", from the other hand it also helps him utilize "Change-focused skills", depending on which skills set is likely to be most effective in a given situation".

Therefore in DBT, the therapist must sometime push aggressively for change and some other time he will let go, instead of continuing his pressure.

The goal is to "ultimately change the patient" and get rid of these "maladaptive solidly ingrained character flaws". This is not an easy but a rather challenging process.

According to Marsha Lineham, the author of this brilliant therapeutic approach, BPD is fundamentally a "disorder of the emotional regulation system".

Masha Lineham considers the "bad behavior" as a consequence of "emotional dysregulation".

This is as mention previously, the way most "Cognitive Behavioral Therapy" work "distorted cognition or belief" trigger some "negative unhealthy emotions" which are often translated into "behavioral catastrophe and disaster".

"Impairment in the ability to regulate emotions" is believed to be the influence of an "invalidating environment" and an "underlying biological vulnerably" to negative emotions.

According to "Lineham's biosocial model of BPD" the "emotional dysregulation" of these individuals raises when they are in an "invalidating environment".

"Pervasive criticism", "minimizing", "trivializing" and "punishing" characterize the "invalidating environment".

In some cases, "some parents pathologize the patient with BPD", with some "socially undesirable and permanent personality traits" such as: "lazy", "slow", "paranoid".

These "qualifications" that are often "unrealistic and misleading", have a profound impact on the patient who end up having "difficulty with trusting his own thoughts and feelings".

As a result he believes what he wants, thinks and what he does is: "inappropriate", "untrue", "unimportant" or is a "reflection" of the "flaws in his personality".

This is an example of the "powerful impact of words on people's believes system", mostly when these words come from someone the patient idolizes or respects such as some parental figures. The is how a "world of words" can affect the patient negatively

That is why it is probably wise to have this as a motto "One must always say what he means, and means what he says" when interacting with these types of patients who are "emotionally disrupted" in order to avoid a disaster.

Rather than trusting their "own internal experiences", the patients with BPD have a tendency to rely on the "social environment", in order to understand "what they should think, feel or do".

This tendency is believed to contribute to their "hypersensitivity to interpersonal stimuli", and their "sensitivity to perceive social rejection" or "fear of abandonment".

In addition, the "invalidating environment" is perceived or conceptualized as likely to "punish or ignore appropriate normal emotional display" like: "sadness in response to losses", "anger in response to the inability to achieve one's goal".

While extreme emotional display are reinforced. This reinforcement of "dramatic or erratic behavior" is thought to "increase the probability of similar behavior".

Patient with BPD by example, may develop a "pattern of threatening suicide", or "engaging in self injurious behavior".

They have learned that "such behavior" sometime result in "their being noticed", "their being understood" and "their receiving nurturance or attention by others".

That is probably why they often engage in a "spell of self-injurious behavior" in order to "get the attention and the nurturance" they long for so intensely to the point that it makes them come across as being "very needy".

It is according to the "biosocial model of BPD", unhelpful to "pejoratively label the patient" as "being manipulative".

Instead the patient is believed to be responding to a "history of intermittent reinforcement of emotional escalation" and an "invalidating environment".

"High emotional vulnerability" can make an already "invalidating environment" even worse.

"Increase invalidation" may further exacerbate

"emotional vulnerability".

As most CBT approaches, the focus of DBT is to change "maladaptive behavior" and "cognitive pattern".

There are "Four Stages in DBT".

During "Stage I" there is a "display of severe behavioral dyscontrol" and "life threatening problems" including: "non-suicidal self injurious behavior" like "cutting and burning". The goal should be the reduction of life threatening and self- injurious behavior. The "life threatening behavior" must be replaced by "skillful behavior".

"Stage II" "Posttraumatic stress" is the focus during this stage. It is being treated by some "exposure therapy protocol" just like patient suffering from "PTSD": ("Post Traumatic Stress Disorder"). Some patient will revert back to the "behavioral dyscontrol" specific of "Stage I" during "stage II"

"Stage III" addresses "problem in living that are not debilitating".

"Stage IV" targets a "sense of completeness", "spiritual growth", "insight", "enhance awareness", "sustained joy" and other fulfilling life endeavors.

As described previously there are four modes of treatment in DBT.

They are as followed:

1) Group skill Training.

2) Individual Therapy.

3) Ad Hoc Phone Consultation

4) Therapists Consultation Team

_"Skill Training" is like a "formal class vs. a traditional Group Therapy". The goal is to acquire new "cognitive and behavioral life skills". The DBT patient indeed needs to learn certain "behavioral, emotional, cognitive and interpersonal skills".

The format of this particular group should be 8-12 members, for a weekly two-hour group sessions with two DBT trained co-leaders.

"The first hour is devoted for homework review for skills learned the previous week". During homework review, Groups members take turn to discuss their success and challenges as well as implementing new skill learned.

"During the second hour new skills are taught didactically and at times experientially from the skills training manual". The work-books provide a series of exercises organized by modules.

"Individual Therapy sessions" are usually done in a standard "out-patient DBT" and are typically 45-60 minutes once a week, to approve and maintain patient's motivation to continue to work toward developing a "Life worth living"

"Telephone Consultation" is mostly to "enhance the skills learned in group-skill training". These are brief telephone calls lasting less than 10 minutes.

"Lastly Consultation Team" is a requirement for DBT's Therapists, to commit to a weekly consultation team. The goal is for the therapists to treat each other using the same DBT principles.

In conclusion DBT is a complex and comprehensive behavioral treatment for patients with "Borderline Personality Disorder" It is a CBT approach designed for Borderline Patient. According to the science behind this, it has been reported this particular CBT approach concocted by Marsha Lineham, has helped numerous patients with Borderline Personality Disorder.

H.C.B

04-23-15

Chapter 14: Sex And Sexual Disorders

_The Influence of Sex on the Human Brain

_The Power of Sex in
intimates relationships

_Sexual Disorders DSM-5 Version

The Influence of sex on the Human Brain

What are the impacts of sexual activity on the Human Brain?

Most of us would be curious to know how sexual activity affects our brain. Having some knowledge about this will perhaps make us better in accomplishing the act and as a result we probably will become a better partner for our mates.

According to some experts on this captivating topic, it is not easy to accomplish any study in this domain and rightly so, since we are talking about a very intimate and private matter.

In some cases some individuals who are part of these studies have to masturbate while they are in the MRI machine.

Understanding how sex affects your brain, not only can improve your participation in the sexual act but also can help you in other areas of your health according to Barry R Komisaruk, PhD a distinguished professor of psychology as Rutgers University In Newark, New Jersey.

Even though this subject is very difficult to tackle, some scientists begin to untangle some of the mysteries around it. One of the conclusions of these studies is the assertion that sex is like a drug. The pleasure we get from sex is mostly due to the release of dopamine, a neurotransmitter that activates the reward center of the brain. This is the same chemical responsible for the euphoria; "the high" people get from drugs. Therefore taking cocaine and having sex involve the same brain region.

Other compounds like methylphenidate, methamphetamine, nicotine, amphetamine, all involve the same area of the brain: the "Nucleus Acumbens" and the "Substantia Nigra". The "Mesolimbic Dopamine System" therefore constitutes an important focal point in the brain reward system. It is also believe that some nuclei of the "Hypothalamus" play a role in sexual response and mating behavior, the fight and flight response and pleasure.

There is a study that reports, women who have sex without a condom have fewer depressive episodes compared to those who have sex with a condom. It seems like these women have benefited from some chemical incorporated in the ejaculate.

Some researchers conclude indeed, that various compounds in the semen including "estrogen" and "prostaglandin" that are absorbed into the body during unprotected sex have some antidepressant properties.

It is also believe that sex has the ability to decrease pain. A study involving people who have migraine or cluster headache, reported a total or partial decrease of the headache after they have sex. It is also believe that women who stimulate an area of the G spot have an elevation of the pain threshold. Some scientists think this phenomenon happens because of the release of oxytocin, which has pain relieve property.

According to another study done with rodents, those who engage in chronic sex once a day for fourteen consecutive days, grew more neurons in the "Hyppocampus", a nucleus which along with the "Amygdala" another nucleus, are part of the "Limbic System" and play a role in learning and memory. The researchers believe that there is a possibility that sex could also boost memory in Human Beings as well.

The same study also found that rats were less stressed when they have sex frequently. This observation has also been reported in Human Beings, since it is being described that people who just had sex respond better to stressful situation. In addition it is also believed that the way sexual intercourse decreases stress is by decreasing the blood pressure.

Finally some groups of researchers endorse the notion that sex is more likely to make men sleepy when compared to women. Their explanation is that, the part of the brain known as "Prefrontal Cortex" which is the decision-making section, wound down after ejaculation. This action of being wind down along with the release of "oxytocin and serotonin", contribute to this occurrence.

The "Prefrontal Cortex" is the executive territory of the brain responsible for planning and decision-making. This region is still immature during teenage years, which is the reason why teen-agers lack the capacity to make sound decisions.

In addition research epidemiologist George Davey Smith of the University of Bristol and Stephen Frankel of Queen's University in Northern Ireland reported in the British Medical Journal, there appears to be a strong relationship between the rate of sexual orgasm and the length of life.

In their study the death rate for the least sexually active men was twice as high as that for the most active. Reflecting on this findings makes one wonders why some people use some street drugs such as: amphetamine, PCP, Cocaine, that have in addition to the same pleasurable effect of releasing dopamine in the reward center of the brain, also affect negatively other areas, so many other regions of the brain causing numerous individuals to become cognitively deficient because of the destruction of some brain structures during a cocaine induced stroke, a cocaine induce seizure or a cocaine induced myocardial infarction. All of these as a result of the direct damages on some part of the brain and the body, done by these chemicals.

H.C.B
06-15-15

The power of sex
in intimate relationships

When we consider the influence of sex on the Human brain, it is fair and logical to say that sex is the food, the nutrient of intimate relationships. When most intimate relationships are not fed properly, they starve and debilitate.

Knowing all the positive impacts of sex on the brain particularly on the hedonic center of this organ, it is not surprising that it is considered an important component of intimate relationships.

Some people would state that it is not always about sex, since we know there are some warm and cozy relationships, which are purely platonic; they therefore do not focus that much on sex.

However in reality this platonic stage could be seen in the early phase of most romances. There are some other ingredients that come to the picture, such as the compatibility of the sexual partners involved.

In order to have the maximum enjoyment from sex, the partners must have much more than a formal attraction to each other, they must have a certain degree of chemistry that makes the process magical.

They must have the compatibility; they must have a certain harmony in order to savor the fruit constituted by the act of sexual possession and devour each other to the fullest.

They also must be patient, hold their horses, restrain their hunger; they must start feeding themselves by attacking their meal slowly from the periphery and slowly directing themselves toward the center if they want to maximize the delight of their hot, spicy and delicious dish. They must start feeding themselves by ingesting the appetizer before feasting on the principal.

They must take their time engaging into their foreplay, dwelling into it and enjoying it, in order to capitalize on their ecstasy later.

H.C.B

11-30-15

Sexual Disorders DSM-5 Version

The "Sexual Disorders" according to the new version of the DSM are listed as followed; "Delayed Ejaculation", "Erectile Disorder", "Female Orgasmic Disorders", "Female Sexual Interest/ Arousal Disorders", "Premature (Early) Ejaculation", "Substances/ medications induced Sexual Dysfunction", "Other Specified Sexual Dysfunctions" and "Unspecified Sexual Dysfunctions".

These sexual disorders may have different subtypes. They may be: "lifelong", "acquired", "generalized" and "situational".

There are also some other factors involved such as: "Partner factor", "Relationship factor", "Individual vulnerability factor", "Psychiatric comorbidities", "Stressors" and "Cultural and Religious factors"

"Partner factor" implies partner sexual problem and partner health status.

"Relationship factor" alludes to poor communication, discrepancies in desire for sexual activity.

"Individual vulnerability factor" relates to poor body image, history of sexual or emotional abuse; "Psychiatric comorbidities" refer to conditions like "depression" or "anxiety"

"Stressors", this particular group alludes to some factors such as job loss and bereavement

"Cultural or Religious factor" like inhibitions related to prohibitions against sexual activity or pleasure, attitude toward sexuality should be listed. "Medical factor" could be relevant to prognosis, course or treatment.

In addition "aging "may be associated with a normal decreased in sexual functions.

Sexual responses could be intermingled by biological, intrapersonal, interpersonal and cultural context. Therefore sexual function involves a complex interaction among biological, sociocultural, psychological factors, relationship distress, and partner's perpetration of violence.

Some medical condition due to pelvic nerve damage can affect sexual activities.

Non-sexual mental disorders, effect of substances drugs or medication should be all ruled out in the diagnostic of sexual dysfunction when the etiology of a sexual problem is unknown.

These are all considerations that should be emphasized and reviewed in the study of sexual disorders according to the new DSM. Based on this new classification, there is wide variety of conditions that could be involved in order to make a diagnosis of sexual disorder.

H.C.B
01-06-16

Chapter 15:
Psychotic Concepts

_Psychosis, Insanity and the Human Mind

_Psychotic Disorders DSMV version

Psychosis, Insanity and the Human Mind

Psychosis is often characterized by: disorganized or catatonic behavior, disorganized speech, sensory distortion of different modality such as auditory, visual, olfactive and tactile hallucinations; delusions which are false and erratic beliefs and negative symptoms like: alogia, anhedonia, amotivation.

Psychosis in other word is a profoundly abnormal process where the psychotic individual is totally out of touch with reality. The psychotic patient lives in world where he misperceives every single entity; he lived in an environment loaded with false unreal components. He lives in a world, which for him is full with demons that haunt him relentlessly, making his life a living hell. In order for him to flee this demonic universe, he would not hesitate to jump from a multiple story building if in his sick mind; he perceives this strategy as his only path to safety. However because of the inaccuracy of his ability to perceive, he may instead end up killing himself or injure himself very badly.

Insanity seems to imply a higher degree in the mind- altering process and can probably be alluded to the psychopath who often engages in a senseless, useless mass or individual killing. This type of scenario has happened so many times before, that it seems like a daily occurrence.

Insanity is an expression of how Human Beings generally have no regard for their fellow human beings, no regard for their life.

Insanity is probably an expression of these hysteric killings happening throughout the world including some countries like Iraq, Afghanistan,

Syria, and the Palestine, to name a few locations where there is a craving for destruction and killing.

Insanity is probably an odd, a bizarre phenomenon when Human Beings are thirsty for the blood and hungry for the flesh of their fellow Human Being as if they were dealing with some sort of Cannibalism.

Insanity is perhaps a reflections of the total chaos, the Mayhem that seems to be everywhere in the world in this twenty first century. It may also be a consequence of the systematic destruction of the human brain by these compounds of abuse, that give people the illusion that they are living in a better world. There may be a connection between these chemicals and the creation and the maintenance of the hellish world where we are living.

This world that most of us seem to accept and take as a dimension of normalcy.

H.C.B

09-07-15

Psychotic Disorders DSMV version

In the chapter on Psychotic Disorders, the new DSM describes some illnesses like "the Schizophrenia Spectrum Disorders", some "other Psychotic Disorders" such as: "Delusional Disorders", "Brief Psychotic Disorder", "Schizophreniform Disorder", "SchizoAffective Disorder" and "Schizotypal Personality Disorder".

The hallmark of these disorders is about five major domains including: "Delusions", "Hallucinations," "Disorganized Thinking" (Speech), "Disorganized Motor Behavior" (Catatonia) and "Negative Symptoms".

"Delusions" are defined as fixed beliefs that are not flexible or changeable, in spite of conflicting evidence. Their content covers a variety of themes such as: "persecutory", "referential", "somatic", "religious", "grandiose", "erotomanic" and "nihilistic".

"Hallucinations" are perceptive experiences occurring without an external stimulus. They could be so vivid and so clear that they may be perceived as normal. A major difference though, is that they are not under voluntary control and the subject affected has no power over them whatsoever. They could occur in any sensory modality. The most common are "auditory hallucinations" usually experienced as voices, are frequently seen in the Schizophrenia Spectrum Disorders. Another important marker associated with them, they usually occur on a clear sensorium

"Disorganized Thinking" is usually referred to the subject's speech, which could be derailed or loose when it is being switched from one topic to the other. It could also be tangential when the answer is completely unrelated to the question asked. It could be completely incoherent or called "gibberish talk" or "Word Salad" when it is severely disorganized or incomprehensible.

"Grossly Disorganized or Abnormal Motor Behavior" may manifest itself in variety of ways from "silliness" to unpredictable "agitation". "Catatonic Behavior" is a marked decrease in reactivity to the environment from "negativism" or resistance to instructions to adopting an inappropriate "rigid or bizarre posture" to "mutism" and "stupor", which is a complete lack of verbal and motor response.

"Negative Symptoms" of emotional expression are the key for the morbidity associated with schizophrenia. A couple of them are particularly prominent in the illness: "diminished emotional expression" and "avolition". This reduction of "emotional expression" may be reflected in the face, the ability to make eye contact, the "intonation of speech" or "prosody" and the "movement of the hands, the head and the face", which usually give an emotional emphasis to speech.

"Avolition" is a decrease in motivated self-initiated purposeful activities. The individual may sit for long period of time and displays little interest in participating in work or social activities.

Some other negative symptoms are "Alogia" or diminished speech output, "Anhedonia" or a decrease ability to experience pleasure, "Asociality" or an apparent lack of interest in social activities often associated with "avolition"

The "nosologic entities" or psychiatric conditions described in this group are as previously mentioned: "Brief Psychotic Disorders", "Schizophreniform Disorders", "Schizophrenia", "Subtance/Medication induced Psychotic Disorders" and "Schizotypal Personality Disorder" which probably should have been listed with the personality disorders.

These are a summary of conditions covered by the new DSM in the chapter dedicated to Psychotic Disorders.

H.C.B
08-12-15

Chapter 16: Mood Disorders And Mood Related Concepts

_Mood Disorders Success and survival

_Mood Disorders DSMV version

Mood Disorders, Success and Survival

The gaging of our mood is important in order to anticipate our chances to succeed or fail.

It is critical to take the pulse of our mood, in order to measure our ability to survive or succumb.

Since when our mood spirals downward toward its somber pole, we have all the components of a "major depressive episode" including: "depressed, sad and discouraged mood", "loss of interest and pleasure", "decreased or increased appetite with craving for sweet or carbohydrate", "insomnia", "psychomotor changes", "decreased energy, tiredness and fatigue", "feelings of worthlessness and guilt", "impaired ability to think" and finally "thoughts of death or suicidal ideation with suicide attempts" in some cases.

However when our mood goes upward we usually have all the ingredients for a manic episode including: "inflated self-esteem or grandiosity", "decreased need for sleep" translated by an increase in our level of energy, we become "more talkative than usual with a certain pressure to keep talking"; we do have some "flight of ideas" with the subjective experience that "our thoughts are racing". We become "easily distracted", we do have some "increase in our ability to have some goal directed activity" and we get "involved excessively in some pleasurable activity".

Our ability for fighting or flying, our aptitude at succeeding or failing are closely related to the quality of our mood.

Henry C. Barbot, M.D.

When we feel depressed and perceive ourselves as being down in the dumps, we usually have no energy, we let ourselves slip into helplessness, and we end up raising the white flag in order to surrender. When on the contrary we feel confident with some inflated self-esteem, we think we are invincible, we believe we can overcome any challenge and ultimately tackle whatever comes along our path.

It is clearly obvious that our "state of mind" or rather the "state or the pulse of our mood" can tell a great deal about our ability to succeed and survive or to fail and succumb

H.C.B
09-26-15

Mood Disorders DSMV version

The chapter dedicated to Mood Disorders in the new DSM covers some entities such as: "Bipolar and Related Disorders", which contrarily to the previous versions of the DSM are separated from the "Depressive Disorders".

It is clear this new version of the DSM is following a path different from the one followed by its predecessors. The Mood Disorders, contrarily to the format of the previous DSM, are not grouped together. "Bipolar Related Disorders" are being placed between the "Schizophrenia Spectrum Disorders" and the "Depressive Disorders". The rational for this, is the fact that they are considered as a bridge between two diagnostic classes in terms of "symptomatology", "family history" and "genetics". "Bipolar and Related Disorders" include: "Bipolar I Disorder", "Bipolar II Disorder", "Cyclothymic Disorders", "Substance/Medication induced Bipolar and Related Disorder", "Bipolar and related Disorder due to another medical condition", "Specified Bipolar and Related Disorder" and "Unspecified Bipolar and Related Disorder".

"Bipolar I Disorder" is considered the classic "Manic Depressive Disorder" or "affective psychosis".

The so called "Bipolar II Disorder" which includes a major depressive episode and an hypomanic episode, is not considered as a so mild a condition as it used to be, mostly because of the depression and the mood instability that prevent the sufferer from functioning.

The "Depressive Disorders DSMV version" include: "Disruptive Mood Dysregulation Disorder", "Major Depressive Disorder", "Persistent Depressive Disorder" (Dysthymia), "Premenstrual Dysphoric

Disorder", "Substance/Medication induced Depressive Disorder", "Depressive Disorder due to another medical condition", "Specified Depressive Disorder" and "Unspecified Depressive Disorder".

"Disruptive Mood Dysregulation Disorder" is characterized by severe recurrent temper outbursts manifested by verbal rage and physical aggression toward people or property, that are grossly out of proportion in intensity or duration to the trigger.

"Major depressive Disorder" is the classic form of the illness, as we know it from the previous versions of the DSM, except that in this version the disorder is a recurrent one, in the majority of cases.

"Premenstrual Dysphoric Disorder" was moved from an appendix of DSM-4 to the second section of DSM-5. This condition begins following ovulation and remits within a few days of menses with a marked impact on functioning.

This is a list of the Mood Disorders as conceived and presented by DSM-5 which is clearly departing from the way the previous versions of the DSM perceived and described them.

H.C.B
08-13-15

Chapter 17: Personal and Professional Matter

_The Sudden Collapse of my Universe

_Is Retirement still a possible
option in this day and age

_My Haitian Journey Vs. My
American Journey

_A self-psychoanalysis: Weakness of
Character or being hostile and wild

The sudden Collapse of my Universe

When I came to this country years ago, my universe collapsed suddenly and I found myself in an all-new and hostile world.

I found myself transitioning, from being a well valued and regarded physician specialized in Internal Medicine practicing in my father's office in Haiti, to a peon carrying a fully loaded bag of parcels on his back, working as a messenger roaming the commercial streets of East side Manhattan in order to give the company for which I was working for, some "Motor Service" as they put it at the time.

At the end of my workday my feet were painfully swollen and I had to dip them in some "Epson Salt" in order to get some relief preparing myself for the agony of the next day.

The universe for which I fought so hard becoming a physician after 7 years of study at the State University of Haiti was gone, it collapsed, vanished at the blink of an eye.

And there I was, in a country where everything was foreign to me, every single entity was unfriendly, intimidating and challenging to me.

I had to deal with a frigid weather, being an unprepared product of the Caribbean Islands.

I had to deal with the "bone chilling temperatures" of this country, me a bonafide "Son of the Sun", a product of the Caribbean islands, a man who never saw any snow or ice before in my life. I was far from being a creature of this frigid cold and frosty weather.

I had to sustain the weird feeling of a milieu, which I perceived as being frankly unfriendly, hostile and unwelcome.

In addition, I had to learn a foreign language, which I perceived as being pure jargon for me; since at the time of my entrance in this country, I could not speak or comprehend any English.

And to make matter worse, I had to face the despairing and depressive feeling of loneliness, after I left behind my wife and my 3-year-old daughter.

And maybe the cruelest of all, I had to regress from being a financially independent man, to becoming an individual fully dependent on his relatives to survive in what I perceived as a jungle at the time.

It was like I suddenly fell in a dark and deep ditch where it was impossible for me to perceive anything around me but a total black out, a peach black environment.

It was like I was in a narrow and lengthy tunnel with no light at its end.

The only hope that kept me driving was the expectation of being reunited soon with my wife and my daughter who were supposed to join me in a few weeks.

This hope was generated by the strong belief that with them at my side, I could make the impossible become possible and beat all the odds.

It has been more than three decades since I had painfully withstood the disastrous fall of my universe.

It was at the time, the conclusion of a chapter of my life, and the commencement of a new one.

It was the expiration of my life in my beloved birth country and the creation of another existence in a new and hostile land

It was in other word the end of my "Haitian Journey" and the beginning of a long and challenging "American Journey".

H.C.B

06-27-15

Is retirement still a possible option in this day and age?

Retirement is a very important milestone in an individual's life. This is probably why one must thoroughly analyze it before jumping into it, in this day and age, since it could be like a double edge sword.

It could possibly be a wonderful time in an individual's life, when he does not feel the pressure of having to go to work day in and day out.

This feeling of being trapped as if one were in jail will be gone. One has the ability to enjoy the view of a sunset after being deprived of this picture for years.

This new perception of being free can produce joy and euphoria initially. This can soon turn sour for a career workaholic like me. It cans soon turns disastrous when boredom starts raising its ugly head and shows up on the horizon. It could become catastrophic when one has no clue about the way to manage it.

It could even become lethal; deadly in a way I could hardly understand. I have seen so many of my colleagues dying mysteriously, inexplicably just a few months after they officially retire. Up to this day I do not fully understand this phenomenon.

Another negative aspect or retirement is that, the simple process of retiring amputates the income by more than half. As a result this could have a profound impact on an individual who is used to a certain life style and find himself suddenly unable to provide the basic for his family.

This could represent a major blow for our self-esteem when we become unexpectedly unable to pay our bills and subsequently powerless at feeding and sheltering our family. In a brief instant we then can be thrown in a world of gloom and hopelessness.

When we consider all these prospects, this important milestone in our life could ultimately lead to a catastrophe.

That is probably why people nowadays keep working deep into their seventies or even their eighties. That is perhaps why the most rational question one must ask before jumping into this phase of life is the following: "Is retirement still a possible option in this day and age"?.

H.C.B

09-23-15

My Haitian Journey vs. My American Journey

My Haitian Journey was reflected in a book entitled: "Experience de Jeunesse a Travers un Petit Pays" that was written in French.

This book is in fact a collection of poems about my life in Haiti, which was also written in French under: "Recueil de Poemes sur Ma Vie in Haiti".

I did also entitle it: "Souvenir D' Antan and Collection de jeunesse", which is another title reflecting a summary of my life in Haiti.

The book is about my prime as an adolescent growing up in Haiti. My youth was loaded with dreams and romance, which should have shaped me as the person I became at the dusk of my life but did not.

In fact, I became profoundly touched over the years and engraved by my professional life as a physician who has been practicing in the field of Psychiatry for more than twenty years.

My American Journey on the other hand was described in another book entitled: "My American Journey" a novel about my life in the United Stated.

I started redacting this manuscript the day of my sixty-first birthday, 30 years after my coming to the US.

I was very thoughtful this particular day, reflecting back on my long journey in this country.

A journey that was initiated approximately 30 years ago maybe more if I take into account my numerous failed attempts to reside here in this country.

Looking back from the time I severed the umbilical cord linking me to my motherland, a land that is still part of the "Third World". A land that is still considered as "under developed" and that was torn over the years by so many natural disasters.

I still remember this time that already seems so far away and so fuzzy in my mind; a time when I ended up frustrating myself and so many people around me.

I still remember my reluctance and my profound anguish at having to make a decision to abandon my birth country in order to pursue a career as a physician in the US.

I still remember all these people who in principle should have cared about me and claimed to have been concerned about my wellbeing.

I still painfully remember perceiving their pressuring me in an attempt to get rid of me, since they did not wish to see me around any longer.

All these individuals, who callously had no regards for my feelings and were on a mission to push me away in order to satisfy their hidden agenda at the time.

All these folks who kept asking me what did I want to do with my life? When will I finally come up with a decision to improve it?

They kept asking me relentlessly what do you want to do with your life?

They did not even realize that their insistence had the impact of making me not give a dam about any future of mine.

The question was asked so many times that it became like a broken record.

I still remember how painful, how agonizing it was for me to sever the umbilical cord attaching me to my country of birth.

All these subjects who should have facilitated the transition for me by taking it easy on me, but were possibly way too scared of my becoming perhaps a monkey on their back, an obstacle an impediment to their own emancipation and the welfare of others more precious and more valuable to them.

When I was finally able to sever the umbilical cord attaching me to my "Alma Mater", it was for me the beginning of a new life full of challenges, full of humiliations, full of dismay; but in the long run, full of satisfaction and full of achievements.

Here I was this faithful day, in a foreign country where every single entity was hostile to me, concocting a cocktail of misery and fabricating a tissue of gloom and despair.

Here I was in an environment, where I had to fight so many adversaries.

One of my enemies was the language, since I could at the time, hardly understand or speak a single English word.

I could not comprehend or hear a single word in the language of Shakespeare.

Another dreaded element was the weather, this frigid weather that made every bone of my body ache in an unbearable way.

Being from a tropical country and therefore "A son of the sun" as I like to say, the sight of the white stuff never came across my visual field before. I never saw a snowfall before I came to this country. I never had to endure the horrendous bite of a frigid weather.

And as if this harsh panorama was not enough, I had to initially be dependent on some family members to feed and shelter me since I was penniless.

When my wife joined me a few weeks later, I was facing and struggling with some new and mixed emotions.

I was elated, delighted that she was finally at my side but I was also preoccupied with her wellbeing and that of my children. Especially since at the time she was very pregnant and near term with our second child in addition from being here with our first progeny.

I was soon exploring the streets of New York, this big city on a daily basis, avidly searching for work. I was in a job-hunting mood while still unable to speak or comprehend the local language.

That was a brutal transition, since a few weeks before I was still in my country of birth, in my father's medical office functioning as a full-fledged physician.

I was addressed with the utmost respect due to my rank. I was then the Godly Dr. Henry C Barbot a physician specialized in Internal Medicine.

And here, in America, I was in some sort of ruthless transition that seemed more like a bad dream, an individual who was demoted to become a peon beating the street of New York.

I was in Manhattan working as a messenger and carrying a heavy bag loaded with parcels to be delivered to different offices throughout a city where I could hardly orient myself.

I had to cover miles and miles of distance on a daily basis delivering my freight.

When I was finally relieved from my daily duty, I headed home with swollen and throbbing feet.

My wife had to nurse me by soaking them in "Epson Salt" preparing me for the next day.

I had to get used to my new routine and bite the bullet, transitioning from being a physician to becoming a blue-collar worker overnight.

I had to keep working at that capacity over a long period of time. And over the years I did assume multiple roles in order to survive.

I have been a messenger, a security guard, a psych-tech, a home attendant, an orderly, a school bus escort and a taxi driver.

I worked assuming the different roles just listed previously, for the next 8 years in order to provide for my family while I was at the same time desperately trying to save my medical career. I had to go for a long and difficult road, rich in sinuosity and loaded with bumps, making the ride strenuous and jagged.

During the first year I spent in the U.S, I passed my English test which was a requirement in addition to my ECFMG (Educational Commission For Foreign Medical Graduate), which I had passed while I was still in Haiti. Once I had these required credentials, I was supposedly ready for an internship and a residency here in this country.

I however had to wait 8 years before I was finally able to access the American medical world. I had to wait for an eternity before I could finally perceive a positive outcome to my life.

I had one year of "Internship in Transitional Surgery" and three years of "Residency Training in Psychiatry".

I became an Attending Psychiatrist in 1993 and I have been working since then in this field for about 22 years.

I am still going strong without any hope of retiring any time soon.

After a short description of My Haitian Journey, this was a summary of my long and agonizing American Journey that is still ongoing.

H.C.B

09-02-15

A self-Psychoanalysis: Weakness of Character, or being hostile and wild.

When I meditate on my mood swing or my being snappy at time, I often ask myself whether this sudden explosive attitude is not masking something else. I ask myself whether I am not unconsciously hiding something different, like a weakness of character or something else such as being overly sensitive.

In an attempt to focus on myself as a way of doing some self-analysis, some self-observing or self-studying; It seems indeed that I come across sometime as if I were possessed by some bad spirit or some "obnoxious loa" which is the usual name given to the voodoo divinities; based on the fact that my mood was so labile that it became close to a state of wilderness.

This projection of wilderness is sometime quite confusing and generally questions my academics and my social interaction.

I intentionally put myself in the spotlight; I purposefully put myself under the lens of a microscope, just because of a comment I overheard someone makes about me years ago, someone who seems to wonder whether an old bear like me, could be educated. I was deeply moved by this assertion, because of my usual perception of myself.

As a human being, I always thought that my being wild and unpredictable is in reality an appearance because I always thought of myself as a sensitive guy, a sensitive guy who usually carries his heart in his hands.

However there is always a certain degree of relativity in everything. Albert Einstein knows a lot about that mostly in a description of his famous theory of "Relativity" which apparently has changed the world.

H.C.B

07-27-15

Chapter 18:
Miscellaneous

_The Fruits of the Haitian Countryside

_The Haitian Industry

_ The Harvest of the Sugar Cane

_Rural Festivity.

_You (Parents)

_Riviere Froide

_The influence of music
on the Human Brain

The fruits of the Haitian Countryside

Our country, being located in the Caribbean produces a wide variety of tropical fruits. These fruits exhibit a diversity of colors including: yellow, red, pink and green to mention just a few.

They indeed display a multitude of tints that remind the shades of a rainbow.

These colors are so vivid they seem to merge with the panorama, projecting therefore a dazzling and marvelous scenario that makes us feel like we are in a surreal magical environment.

These tropical fruits are so fragrant, so sweet that simply laying eyes on them triggers an abundance of saliva in our mouth; a sign that we usually have a enormous craving, a immense desire to feast on these Caribbean products.

We are alluding to some fruits as juicy as the mango, sometime the pineapple or the apricot, the papaya, the grenadine and the oranges.

Regardless of their individual characteristics they seem to have formed a united front, when we talk about tropical fruits.

They are so unique not only by their appearance and their taste, but also the location where they originate, which reminds us of a magical environment, a paradise that is frequently coveted not only by the inhabitants of the locality but also by some strangers visiting the region.

A paradise located on earth that is quite accessible and could be the ideal place for vacation.

Henry C. Barbot, M.D.

This multitude of fruits some more delicious than the others, are all the products of our rich magnificent birth country: Haiti the pearl, the most cherished gem of this group of islands.

It is also very suitable to know that all these agricultural products come from this beautiful Caribbean island, which is also the cadet of the West Indies.

H.C.B

09-28-15

The Haitian Industry

Our country produces a wide variety of food materials such as coffee, sugar cane, chocolate, corn and manioc, to name a small group.

Being a third world country, we are deprived of all these technologies that are so numerous in the industrialized nations.

We have to exploit our modest, original and very creative "Petite Industry".

As I previously mentioned, Haiti as a rule is not an industrialized but mostly an agricultural country; we do have however a small, a tiny industry that is quite peculiar, quite original in its class.

This originality comes from the mills, which are some sort of chatterbox moving with the power of winds that becomes similar to a engine impacting their fan shaped gears.

These Chatterboxes in their daily labor refine the gross products of our countryside, in order for the populace to enjoy the finish goods.

Our mills, our chatterboxes are the main machineries of our "Mini Industry", producing some invigorating delicious black coffee, some crude or refined sugar, and some flour.

This flour is one of the main ingredients of our breads and our tiny biscuits or "biscuits ti beurre", which is a common denomination for them at home in Haiti.

These biscuits with their aroma, that teases our nostrils when they are freshly delivered to the bakery and are still warm. They do have the potential to provoke an inundation in our mouth, by teasing our taste buds as well, reflecting our irresistible desire to have a bite of these delicacies.

H.C.B

10-03-15

The harvest of the sugar cane

Today is a great day for the inhabitants of our countryside.

This is the day for harvesting the sugar cane, a day they have been waiting for the entire year has finally arrived.

Our people, our laborers seem excited.

There is a feverish agitation in our plains.

This is the day, the time to harvest the sugar cane.

Since 4: oo am, at the crack of dawn everyone, including women and children, wake up, leave their plaits these braided fiber couches behind and get out of their huts.

They all make sure they sharpen their machetes in a hurry by using some beautiful rocks of a greyish tint designed for this purpose.

Then follows a jubilant rush towards the sugar cane fields in order to start this important day, the day of the harvest of sugar cane, the main component of their agricultural economy.

Under the multiple bites of the machete's sharp edges, the sugar cane stems seem to leap and form some large piles in a matter of minutes.

They are stacked up in packs and placed in some carriages as soon as these become available to take them away.

And like a choir, our harvesters start humming some creole melodies in the fresh air of the morning.

These creoles melodies are divulged with a mixture of joy and sadness but mostly with a ceremonial air reminding of our African Ancestors and their long and painful moments in the sugarcane fields during the horrendous time of slavery.

Today is a great day for the inhabitants of our plains. This is the time for them to savor the product of weeks of hard and painful labor, preceding the final harvest.

Today is a wonderful day for them since the time for harvesting has finally arrived.

This is the exciting time of the harvest of the sugar cane.

H.C.B

10-03-15

Our Rural Festivities

Ordinarily the people of our countryside, the populaces of our suburbs, organize yearly a "Kaladja" the local denomination for the festivity planned for the celebration of the saint symbolically representing the area.

During this opportunity, there is usually a collective jubilation and the representatives of the neighborhood districts, come in large crowds in order to contribute to the celebration.

They start gathering in the early morning, forming some small groups at the crack of dawn.

They start guzzling some of our local spirit, our delicious "clairin" or "tafia" which is the native alcoholic beverage, our good old and delicious "grogue".

They begin their debauchery at the sound of the drums and the "bamboo".

These Bamboos that emit some voluptuous and lascivious sounds reminding of these groups so popular in Haiti named "Rara" that roam the streets of the locality followed by our elated provincials in hordes, while deeply engrossed and captivated by their dirty and lascivious dancing.

Some of them hang on to some splendid "griffones" (our locale feminine deities) who typically are very attractive with the voluptuously designed curves of their anatomy. They are "bien en forme" like some of us enjoy saying in Haiti, in order to describe these attractive features including the sensual curves of their voluptuous body.

In the evening the crowd seems to enjoy the terrific rhythm of our "Mini Jazz", the musical bands formed by our youths.

They engage in some dancing exhibitions that last all night long.

At some point later, intoxicated by the alcoholic beverages, the music and the "Marabous" our black females deities, the feast continues until dawn at the satisfaction of most people in the community.

This is usually the way our populaces enjoy our rural festivities as per the heritage of our Africans Fathers.

H.C.B

10-03-15

NB: The following poem is about certain parents in Haiti in the late 60's and their behavior toward their children; and how their being different could have had a positive impact on our land.

You (Parents)

You, who always have been hiding behind a wall caring only about your comfort and a cozy space you seem to deeply enjoy just by yourself; showing no regard for sharing it with anyone.

You, who have always been engrossed in your egoism; being in a place that seems to make you dizzy forcing you to exhibit your grandiosity and the might of your ego.

You, who are in a universe loaded with mysteries and oddities; a counterfeit, bogus world made at the dimension of your ambition.

You, who have pushed us miles away by your inability to comprehend and connect with us.

All you have done, all you have accomplished is erecting a wall that seems impenetrable and ends up keeping us further apart.

Do you think you will be able to resolve everything by your stupid rules?

These rules that you usually are the first to violate making you, converting you in moralists deprived of morality.

Do you think you can magically attract us by your absurd and hypocritical guidelines?

Do you believe your pseudo conservatism will tame us?

On the contrary, all it did is irritate, exasperate us. Making us as a result more distant.

All it did is irate and push us further away;

because of its being obsolete.

It is outdated and makes us feel nauseated.

Why don't you try a different strategy, a more rational approach?

Why don't you try to get closer to us?

Why don't you try to be our friends?

May be some understanding will be generated, may be some reconciliation, some compromise will be born; may be something, anything better than what we have will come up.

We are not asking you to tolerate any anarchy; we are not asking you to accept any depravation, any debauch or any corruption.

All we are asking for, is some bonding, some connection.

So we would feel attached to you, we would have the feeling that we can depend on you.

This would have created some sentiment of attachment, some feeling of closeness.

You would have generated some feelings of trust from our part. This probably would have made us think that you have our back.

We would have possibly become a real family; we could have joined forces and cooperate.

May be we could have shared our enthusiasm.

May be we could have combined our intelligence, our motivation, our spiritual and material assets.

And at last we could have been useful to our beloved country.

And above all, we perhaps could have removed it from its underdeveloped status.

H.C.B
Translated from French
10 -24-15

Riviere Froide

There are a multitude of amazing little corners in Haiti.

The region of "Riviere Froide" is famous for its being known as a heaven on earth.

It is indeed a marvelous little corner where usually a soft breeze caresses the green vegetation around it that looks more like a wall protecting this blissful site, which is often the preference of our paramours, the numerous lovers of our land.

Placed in the middle of this fairy, this resplendent location, a river runs its clear and cold water.

This is our sweet, our marvelous "Riviere Froide", Renowned for witnessing so many concubines.

Notorious for seeing so many romances,.

Famous, for viewing all these lovers who have been enjoying this area of dream as their region of predilection, in order to exhibit their lascivious and sensual display.

This river rests its body lazily as if it realizes that the passage of time has no impact on its survival.

As if it realizes indeed that the time passing by has no influence on its resplendent beauty, its amazing magnetism, its fascination and all its appeals that have remained unchanged over the centuries.

It is like this creek, magically recognizes that so many days, so many weeks, so many months and so many years have pass by and all these different components of time have no impact on its existence.

It continues to lay there, insensitive to the passage of time, unaffected by any element that seemingly reflects some animation around it.

It spreads itself out blissfully, inviting the lovers of our cities to joint its flanks made of delight and ecstasy.

These flanks that have entertained so many generations of lovers over the years.

H.C.B
Translated from French
10-24-15

The influence of Music
on the Human Brain

We often feel jubilant, euphoric after we listen and hum a melody we really like and long for.

It is as if we instinctively know how it could have flipped our mood in the blink of an eye, when we perceive ourselves as being glum, unhappy and despondent.

Knowing how music could affect our brain shed some light allowing us to understand this phenomenon and comprehend the benefit of "Music Therapy" for some of our patients.

It is really amazing to see how music could impact the human brain.

It is reported that music helped Thomas Jefferson write the declaration of independence.

It is also reported that when he could not figure out the right wording for a certain part, he would play his violin to help him.

It is also reported that music was the key for Albert Einstein to become one of the smartest men who ever lived.

He says that the reason he was so smart is because he played the violin. One of his friends stated that the way he figures out his problems and equations was improvising on his violin.

Music in reality affects different parts of the Human Being, not just the brain.

It decreases blood pressure and enhances the ability to learn.

It does affect the amplitude and the frequency of brain waves.

It affects breathing rate, blood pressure, and heart rate.

It changes people mood and strengthens or weakens emotions from certain event.

Some music can indeed make people tearful while some other can provoke an eruption of delight and total ecstasy.

The power of music to affect memory is quite fascinating as well. It is reported that Mozart's music activates the left and the right brain. The simultaneous impact on the right and the left-brain maximizes learning and retention.

It is believed that the information being studied activates the left-brain while the music itself activates the right brain.

Activities, which engage both sides of the brain at the same time such as playing an instrument or singing, cause the brain to be more capable to process information.

Learning potential could be increased up to five times by using certain kinds of music.

A simple way students can improve tests score, is by listening to certain type of music before taking a test

High school students who study music are believed to have higher grade point average than those who don't.

Music as a rule is believed to have been processed, by many different areas of the brain.

Among the areas involved, the "sensory cortex" gives some tactile feedback from playing an instrument and dancing.

The "motor cortex" is involved in movement; foot tapping dancing and playing an instrument.

The "auditory cortex" is part of the first stage of listening to sound and the perception and analysis of tone

The "prefrontal cortex" is about creation of expectation, violation and satisfaction of expectation.

The "nucleus accumbens" and the "amygdala" are the major components of the center for emotional reaction of human beings to music.

Some other region such as the "hippocampus" is an integral part of the memory for music, musical experiences and contexts.

A zone such as the "Visual cortex" plays a role in reading music, looking at a performer or monitoring one's own movement.

The "cerebellum" which is a major center for equilibrium is involved in foot tapping, dancing and playing an instrument as well as some emotional reaction to music.

The descriptions of the areas described previously as well as their functions were made possible by the marvels of functional brain imaging.

It is believed that there are two kinds of emotion related to music, a "perceived emotion" in addition to a "felt emotion".

Music can sometime help define some personality traits and probably can be used for the study of personality disorders.

Another fascinating aspect of music is that it can maximize our stamina when we work out, listening to music can drown out, shut down our brain cry for fatigue.

As our body realizes that we are tired and wants to stop exercising, it sends signal to the brain to stop for a break.

However listening to music competes for our brain attention and helps minimize or neutralize the signals alerting our brain of our being tired.

The human brain processes the experience of listening to music in two different ways.

Certain experts consider human beings as having two brains because of the two hemispheres, which are connected by the "corpus callosum" differ in their functions and operate as if they were two diverse brains.

The "left hemisphere" is specialized in "speech activity" while the "right one" is specialized for many "non-linguistic functions".

It is believed that the "left hemisphere" is for propositional, analytic and serial processing of incoming information while the "right one" is more adapted for the perception of appositional, holistic and synthetic relations.

The "right side of the brain" deals with images and imagination, daydreaming, color, parallel processing, face recognition, pattern of map recognition and the perception of music.

The "left side of the brain" deals with logic, language, reasoning, numbers, linearity and analysis.

These differences between the two brains clearly reflect the traditional dualism of "intellect" versus "intuition", "science" versus "art" and "logical" versus "mystery".

Therefore "artists and musicians" use different halves of the brain when compared to "lawyers and engineers".

It is also believed that Einstein and other scientists are "left brain dominant" while Mozart and other artistic people are "right brain dominant".

Henry C. Barbot, M.D.

However it is believed above all that the greatest human potential can only be realized by the use of both sides of the brain.

In spite of the fact the importance of the right hemispheres is greatly emphasized in music. "Musical skills" however form a mixed set, some of which require "left hemisphere integrity" while some require "right hemisphere functioning".

Research has shown that neither cerebral hemisphere is totally dominant for music since both of them are deeply involved.

H.C.B

11-04-15

SPECIAL THANKS TO

I thank God for giving me the will power, the stamina and the humility to write this third book.

I am also grateful to my wife, my children, my parents, my great aunt, my brother in law, my sisters and some of my colleagues particularly Dr. Allen Gore.

I am very appreciative to all these individuals who have been supporting me and encouraging me to complete this project.

ABOUT THE AUTHOR

Dr. Henry Claude Barbot is a graduate of the State University of Haiti. He completed his residency training in internal medicine at the State University Hospital and later completed his training in psychiatry in America. Barbot is a Diplomat of the American Board of Psychiatry and Neurology, the American Society of Clinical Psychopharmacology, the American Board of Addiction Medicine and the American Board of Disability Analysts. He has been writing poetry in French, his native language, since he was a teenager. He started writing about the human mind specifically when he initiated his residency training in Psychiatry.

REFERENCES

_ DSM-5
   Diagnostic and Statistical Manuel of Mental Disorders
   Fifth Edition
   American Psychiatric Association

_ROMHP "Reflection and Opinions of a Mental Health Professional"
   Henry C. Barbot, M.D.

_ROMHP2 "Reflections and opinions of a Mental Health Professional 2"
   Henry C. Barbot, M.D.

_Audio Digest Foundation
   Management of Sleep Disorders
   Audio Digest Psychiatry
   Volume 43, Issue 15
   August 7, 2014

_ Journal of Biological Psychiatry
   Biological aspect of Depression and Suicide
   Carmen Blake, Brian J Miller

_ Journal of Clinical Psychiatry News
   Transcranial Near- Infrared Therapy,
   A new neuro-modulation technic for Depression
   Debra L Beck

Printed in the United States
By Bookmasters